THE SOUL
WHENCE AND WHITHER

The soul has no birth, no death,
no beginning, no end. Sin cannot
touch it, nor can virtue exalt it.
Neither can wisdom open it, nor
can ignorance darken it. It has
always been, and always it will be.
This is the very being of man, and
all else is its cover, like a globe
on the light.
The soul's unfoldment comes from
its own power, which ends in its
breaking through the ties of the
lower planes.
It is free by nature, and looks
for freedom during its captivity.
All the holy beings of the world
have become so by freeing the soul,
its freedom being the only object
there is in life.

Hazrat Inayat Kahn
in *Metaphysics*

THE SOUL
WHENCE AND WHITHER

BY
HAZRAT INAYAT KHAN

EAST-WEST PUBLICATION

© This edition 1984 Nekbakht Foundation
34 Rue de la Tuilerie
92150 Suresnes
France

Distributed by
East-West Publications (UK) Ltd.
Jubilee House
Chapel Road
Hounslow
Middlesex TW3 1TX

ISBN 0 85692 134 3

Typeset in Great Britain by
Tellgate Ltd., London N6 5HX
Printed and bound in Great Britain
by Billing & Sons Limited, Worcester.

TABLE OF CONTENTS

FOREWORD TO THE PRESENT EDITION

'THE Soul-Whence and Whither' is the title of a series of lectures given in 1923 in Suresnes, France, by Pir-o-Murshid Hazrat Inayat Khan during the summer school of the Sufi Movement. This is the first time a complete revision of its text has been attempted, drawing for this purpose on original documents.

The institution of the long summer meetings, bringing together a small number of members, began in 1921 at Wissous (France) where Hazrat Inayat Khan was then living. In 1922 the meetings, still on a small scale, continued at Suresnes. They were followed by another session in September of the same year in the Dutch town of Katwijk where Hazrat Inayat Khan gave a series of lectures on 'The Inner Life'. From the year 1923, when the so-called Summer School began to be better organized and to gather a growing number of interested persons, Hazrat Inayat Khan continued to centre his lectures on a particular subject. This is the way in which all his later books came about.

Between the 2nd of July and the 1st of August 1923 Hazrat Inayat Khan delivered ten lectures on 'The Body', 'The Mind' and 'The Soul' under the heading 'Metaphysics'. On the 10th of August, 1923, he began three series of lectures respectively entitled 'The Soul Towards Manifestation', 'The Manifested Soul' and 'The Soul towards the Goal' which became Part I, II and III of 'The Soul – Whence and Whither', the lectures on 'Metaphysics' being included in Part II. These series were completed on the 19th of September, the last day of the Summer School, on which day he delivered what has become the Introduction and the Conclusion to this work.

An examination of the original documents shows that Miss E.M. Green, Representative at that time of the Sufi Movement in England, prepared the text for publication with the aid of a report taken down by Mrs. G. LLoyd.

Hazrat Inayat Khan revised certain sentences and terms used in his lectures and added a number of new ones. Some six months later, in May 1924, the first edition of the book – which was then entitled 'The Soul-Whence and Whither' – was brought out. .

On receipt of the first copy, Hazrat Inayat Khan wrote the following letter to Miss J.E. Dowland (Nargis) who used to handle the business side of the Sufi publications:

May 27th

My trusted Mureed,

I was very pleased to see the new book. It is got up nicely indeed. Only I am sorry to find a mistake left in the Conclusion.

It is not a journey in truth. Instead of that it is said on the contrary. I hope you will try to do something to correct that mistake with ink or a rubber stamp, to add the word 'not'.

As far as we know it was too late for Miss Dowland to follow this request. The first edition showed: 'It is a journey in truth', whereas Hazrat Inayat Khan had said during the course of his lecture: 'What is this journey taken by the soul? . . . Is it a journey or is it not a journey? It is a journey in fact and *not* a journey in truth'. He also wrote in a copy of the newly printed book after 'Is it a journey or is it not a journey?', 'It is not a journey objectively'. This copy was sent to Miss L. Goodenough who was then responsible for collecting, keeping and reproducing the Master's teachings. She revised the whole text amending a number of other mistakes. In 1927 a second edition was brought out rectifying many of the previous faults, but Miss Goodenough left a note stating that a new publication of the book 'made with a new manuscript' was desirable.

In 1960 Barrie and Rockliff (London) republished the text of the first edition 'for International Headquarters of the Sufi Movement Geneva', but amended the incorrect wording in the Conclusion to read: 'It is not a journey in truth'. There were several reprints. In 1977 a further publication was made by Sufi Order Publications (New York), copying the text of the first edition as it had originally stood. Both of these publications overlooked the revisions carried out in the second edition.

If an attempt is made to-day to understand how so many

errors slipped into the written text, the short time of preparation and the lack of organization involved in reporting the lectures should be borne in mind. Several persons took down Hazrat Inayat Khan's words as he delivered them, the most accurate notes being those of Miss J.E.D. Furnee in shorthand and those of Miss L. Goodenough in longhand, which reports are almost identical. No one, however, made a complete record of all the lectures, or if this was done it has not so far come to light.

A verbatim account of Hazrat Inayat Khan's exact words, based on the various original notes taken down of his lectures, is kept in the archives of the 'Nekbakht Stichting' Foundation (Suresnes, France).

This new publication of 'The Soul – Whence and Whither' attempts to restore omissions, rectify errors and come closer to the Master's style and manner of teaching. The earlier arrangement, assembling into chapters a number of lectures that do not always form a logical whole, has been abandoned. The lectures are now presented separately, with a date, and are followed by questions and answers. This procedure allows each chapter to stand on its own as a complete teaching in itself, and it reproduces the way in which Hazrat Inayat Khan's talks – usually referred to as 'lessons' – were given.

No questions and answers had been included in the first two published versions of the book, but a few of them appeared in the 1923 and 1924 issues of the magazine 'Sufism', edited by Miss E.M. Green. Exact and complete records of the Questions and Answers are often not available, for while Hazrat Inayat Khan's spoken words could be taken down accurately during his lectures, this was not always the case with the exchange of the questions and answers. His questioners were not always well acquainted with the English language, and the answers they received must have been given in a much quicker tempo than the 'lessons'. But in spite of this it has proved possible to reconstruct the contents of the questions and answers to an acceptable degree after comparing all records known to be in existence.

On the whole the questions have a close connection with

the lecture and are useful in elucidating difficult points. Sometimes they disclose a questioner's personal concern, but Hazrat Inayat Khan always brought attention back to the essence of the problem, and often a question inspired him to develop a subject more fully in the 'lesson' that followed.

Sometimes questions concerning the day's lecture were put to him on a later occasion following a talk on another subject. Where this has happened, those questions and answers have been added after the lecture to which they pertain.

Some questions – although relevant to a point raised in the 'lesson' – brought answers that followed a side track to the principal subject. These have been placed for preservation in the Appendix, so as not to distract attention from the main theme or disturb its logical order. Readers may be as interested in them as was the original questioner. The Appendix also includes an earlier lecture by Hazrat Inayat Khan on Reincarnation, as this subject is referred to only briefly in the text of the book itself.

A brief observation on the words used by Hazrat Inayat Khan could perhaps be made here. The Master had to speak in a Western language which was very different from his own (Urdu), and which did not have an adequate mystical and metaphysical vocabulary in which he could express the subtle and profound knowledge he wished to impart. At first the terms 'plane', 'sphere', 'world', and even 'heaven' were used indiscriminately by him in his talks, but later an effort was made to connect 'heaven' with the angels, 'sphere' with the djinns, and 'plane' with the earth. He often borrowed words commonly used in science and philosophy in another sense, such as 'intelligence', 'consciousness', and 'mind'; others such as 'electricity', 'magnetism', 'atom', 'sun', 'planet' were often used as vehicles to express an inner meaning. If one does not listen carefully and with an open mind to the explanation he gives, one can be puzzled and easily led astray.

Words like 'nirvana', 'maya', 'pala' (cf. resp. pp. 16, 87-8, 127) are interpreted according to his own view, which has nothing to do with etymology or linguistics. Hazrat Inayat Khan was struck by the sound of the words. Language for him was a simplification of music and in the words he saw hidden music.

One could also find in this book explanations which at first sight seem contradictory and perhaps discouraging to an intellectual mind accustomed to the precise definitions of modern science and philosophy. Hazrat Inayat Khan, however, was a mystic and an artist: he tried to explain what he knew to be true, because it was his own experience. 'I do not give you my ideas; what I give you is my personal knowledge'. (Vadan) And: 'If your mind cannot understand, your soul can understand' is his reply on page 0. The story of the soul told in this book is to be understood essentially by our soul. What is our soul? How can we realize its existence? Hazrat Inayat Khan tries to make this intelligible; but in order to know our soul we must go through a process of lifting the many veils under which we have hidden it. This is the whole Sufi training, and it is explained throughout all Hazrat Inayat Khan's teachings.

One manner of this training, one exercise is called 'unlearning'. This means not only abandoning preconceived ideas or premature judgments, but also considering ideas, objects, persons, customs, institutions, etc. from a new point of view – in the same way as the blind man who wished to see an elephant had to walk around it touching it on different sides. It is through this process of unlearning that one will become able to take in the new notions Hazrat Inayat Khan imparts to readers of his work.

The vision of the soul and its journey, of the construction of the body and the mind that garb the soul – if studied, imagined and meditated on in this way – opens up a new view on everyday life of man in the world. The expansion of his consciousness, the widening of his horizon make him finally all-embracing and conscious of the spark of the divine being in every person. The purpose that Hazrat Inayat Khan shows to each human being born on earth is to tend towards perfection; this is the discovering of the soul.

'The uncovering of the soul is the discovering of God.' (p. 128)

Suresnes, July 1984   ELISE GUILLAUME – SCHAMHART
staff member of the 'Nekbakht Stichting' Foundation

ACKNOWLEDGEMENTS

In the preparation of this book I am greatly indebted to our much loved friend Wazir van Essen for his encouragement, for his reading of the manuscript and for the valuable advice he was able to give me on it before his passing.

My thanks are also due to Miss Joyce Best who, besides assisting in the writing of the Foreword and the Notes, went over the whole text with me. While respecting Hazrat Inayat Khan's original words she made those small revisions always found to be necessary when talks are turned into a written book.

Then I should mention the inestimable help received from the 'Soefi Stichting Inayat Fundatie Sirdar' (The Hague, Netherlands). H.P. Baron van Tuyll van Serooskerken not only recorded many of Hazrat Inayat Khan's lectures together with questions and answers, but also some of his own questions put to the Master privately. The answers were nearly always dictated to him, and with the consent of the above Foundation, those answers have been included in this new publication.

Acknowledgements should be made also of some amendments to the text submitted by Mrs. L. Witteveen-de Vries Feyens while translating the present text into Dutch.

Finally I wish to thank Mrs. E. van Tricht-Keesing for her useful suggestions in the making of the Index.

E.G.S.

INTRODUCTION

19th September, 1923, 3.30 p.m.

BEFORE manifestation what existed? *Dhāt*, the essence of Being, the truly Existing, the Only Being. In what form? In no form. As what? As nothing. The only definition that words can give is: as the Absolute. In Sufi terms this existence is called *Aḥadiyyah*.[1]

A consciousness arose out of this Absolute, a consciousness of existence. There was nothing of which the Absolute could be conscious – only of its existence. This stage is called *Waḥdah*[1]. Out of this consciousness of existence a sense developed, the sense: I exist. It was a development of the consciousness of existence. It is this development which formed the Ego, the Logos, which is termed *Waḥdāniyyah*[1] by the Sufis. With the feeling of I-ness the innate power of the Absolute, so to speak, pulled itself together, in other words concentrated on one point. Thus the all pervading radiance formed its centre, the centre which is the divine Spirit, or the *Nūr*, in Sufi terminology *Arwāḥ*[1]

This centred light then divided existence into two forms: light and darkness. In point of fact there is no such thing as darkness, there has never been darkness. There is only more light compared with less light. This light and darkness formed *ākāsha*[2], or in Sufi terms *asmān*[2], an accommodation, a mould; and the phenomenon of light and shade working through this mould furthered the manifestation into a great many accommodations, *asmāns* or *ākāshas*, one within the other, and one over the other. Every step manifestation has taken has resulted in a variety of forms made by the different substances which are produced during the process of spirit turning into matter. The working of this process has been according to the law of vibration, which is the secret of motion[3]. It is the plane of definite forms of nature which is called by the Sufis *Ajsām*[1]

Out of these forms came gradually from the mineral the vegetable kingdom, from the vegetable the animal kingdom and from the animal the human race, *insān*[1], thus providing for the divine Spirit – *Arwāḥ* – the bodies – *ajsām* – which it has needed from the time it centred itself on one point and from there spread its rays as various souls. Thus six definite steps towards manifestation are recognized by the Sufis. The first three are called *tanzīh* and the next three *tashbīh*[4]. The first three are imperceptible and the next three distinguishable.

There has also been the phenomenon of four elements, besides one which is the source and goal of all elements: *nūr* – the ether – making them five; *bād* – the air –, *ātesh* – the fire –, *āb* – the water –, *khāk* – the earth –. These elements have worked in consonance with one another and against one another in order to bring about the results desired by the divine wisdom working behind them. In every *ākāsha* or *asmān* they have been present more or less. One without the other did not exist, the four together brought the fifth. In this way the whole manifestation took place through a gradual process of development.

Manifestation finished half its task in the creation of man, in whom is born the wisdom of controlling and utilizing all that is on the earth to its best advantage. In man the purpose of manifestation is fully accomplished, especially in such a one as has on his return journey become more and more conscious of the purpose, by widening his outlook and by living a fuller life – the man who has reached that stage of realization which is called divinity, and in which is the fulfilment of the purpose of the whole manifestation.

> Is not the first condition of God's consciousness, which is unconscious, impossible for the human mind to grasp?
>
> Certainly it is but it is possible for the soul to understand it. If it were not so the revelation would not have been vouchsaved. Revelation comes not only as an inspiration but it comes as a soul's experience. Therefore, for the mind it is impossible to understand but for the soul it is its own experience.
>
> Was there ever a period when there was no consciousness in the Absolute Being of God? No life anywhere?

Silent consciousness. We cannot call silent consciousness no consciousness. If there was no consciousness there would never have been a consciousness. It was the development of the consciousness of the Only Being which brought the Self-consciousness. Out of the deep consciousness the Only Being arose and came to Self-consciousness. He became conscious of consciousness.

As thought necessitates movement and mental action, it is difficult to see how it arose in the Absolute before the manifestation.

In the Absolute thought did not arise. It was consciousness which was its predisposition, which was in it, in its being. That consciousness woke, just like a person who is asleep. It is his nature to wake up, he wakes up from sleep.

And God woke up and His waking was the first impulse towards manifestation. That distinct impulse is called *Waḥdah*. But to understand these two distinct planes is rather a difficult thing, because the difference between *Waḥdah* and *Waḥdāniyyah* is very fine and delicate. To become conscious is one thing; to become Self-conscious is another thing. When a sleeping person is just a little awake, a little noise will tell him something is going on. Still he is not self-conscious yet; that comes when he is wide awake:

Waḥdah – when the Absolute became conscious.
Waḥdāniyyah – when the Absolute became wide awake and felt His being as 'I am'. That action brought about that power of breathing in, that is pulling oneself together. As soon as He thought 'I am', He became a conscious existence for Himself as 'I am'. Therefore it is the Logos.

Before manifestation did not the Being of God exist as a trinity in unity?

Before manifestation the Being of God existed as all, all was in it: unity, trinity, duality, non-duality –

11

but not distinct. If it was not there, how would it have come? It all existed, but beyond and above – what existed? God, the Only Being. The knowledge of two, three, four, five is for us, for our benefit, to help us to understand things better, but the natural knowledge is the knowledge of unity, of One, the Only Being.

Were the four elements part of manifestation, or part of the life of the Only Being?

They are all the outcome. Duality is the outcome of manifestation. In origin there is only unity, oneness. All duality in any form is manifestation.

We hear them spoken of as great beings[5]

They are great beings, because they are great powers working through all planes of existence and playing their part in every form.

What is outside the *ākāsha* in which the universe is contained?

Intelligence, which is the light of life, which is the essence of the Whole Being.

PART I

The Soul Towards Manifestation

(Chapters 1–13)

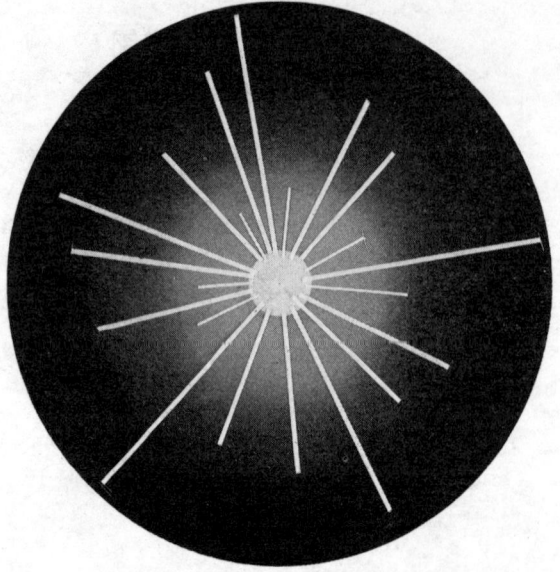

Souls are the rays of this sun, which is called in Sanskrit Brahma. The nature of the ray is to extend and withdraw, to appear and disappear. *(page 16)*

If we study the light and the flames we shall find that all the rays do not go evenly. Some go very far, others remain very near the flame. Every ray, large or small, has a different distance to which it reaches. *(page 22)*

The soul is the ray of the sun which is the Infinite Spirit. The ray is an action of the sun, which is the ray itself. It manifests and returns just as man inhales and exhales. *(page 114)*

CHAPTER 1

10th August, 1923, 5.30 p.m.

THE divine Spirit is known by the mystics of all ages as the Sun, and therefore in all ancient mystical symbols the sun has been pictured as the sign of God. This conception gives further help in the knowledge of metaphysics. This Sun is that aspect of the Absolute God in which He begins to manifest and His first step towards manifestation is contraction, that contraction which is seen in all living beings and in all objects. It is first contraction that takes place and next expansion, which comes as a matter of course, as a reaction. The former tendency is the desire of inhalation and the latter exhalation. The contraction and expansion seen in all aspects of life comes from God Himself.

The omnipresent[6] Light by this tendency becomes concentrated and it is this concentrated Light of Intelligence which is the Sun recognized by the mystics. Shams-e-Tabriz mentions this in his verse[7]: 'When the sun of His countenance became manifest, the atoms of both worlds began to appear. As His light fell every atom donned a name and a form.' The Hindus have called it in the Vedanta *Chaitanya*, the Spirit or the Light of God. In the Qur'an it is mentioned: 'We have made thy light out of Our Light, and of that Light We have made the whole universe.' In plain words this explains that when there was nothing – no form, no name, no person, no object – there was Intelligence. It is the contraction of that Intelligence which brought its essence into a form of Light, which is called the divine Spirit, and the expansion of the same Light has been the cause of the whole manifestation.

The manifestation is the exhalation of God, and what is called by Hindus *pralaya* – destruction or the end of the world – is absorption, which is the inhalation of God. The divine Spirit spreads Itself, which we call the manifestation containing various names and forms, and God contracts Himself, which humanity dreads and calls destruction[8]. For this many blame God, many judge Him and many think it unfair on the part of God to create and to destroy. But for God, Who is the Only

Being, this is the natural condition by which He eternally lives. The beginning and the end of the world is only His one Breath, the duration of which is numberless years. During this one Breath myriads of beings have been born, have lived and died and experienced this world and the next.

Souls therefore are the rays of this Sun, which is called in Sanskrit *Brahma*. The nature of the ray is to extend and withdraw, to appear and disappear and the duration of its existence is short when compared with the durability of the eternal God, the divine Spirit. There are living creatures, small germs, worms and insects which live no longer than a moment, and there are other beings whose life is of a hundred years, and some creatures live longer still. And yet, even if it were a thousand years, it is a moment compared with eternity.

The time that man knows is in the first place discerned by the knowledge of his own physical constitution. The Sanskrit word *pala* which means moment can be seen in the pulse which beats, in pulsation. This knowledge has been completed to some extent by the study of nature, the changes of the seasons and the journeys the Earth makes around the sun. Many wish to limit divine law to this man-made conception of time and they make speculations about it, but the tendency of the mystic is to bend his head low in worship, as the thought of the eternal life of God, the Only Being, comes to his mind. Instead of questioning why and what, he contemplates the Being of God and so raises his consciousness above the limitations of time and space, thus liberating his soul by lifting it to the divine spheres.

> What relation to the great Breath does the destruction of form have during the manifestation? Does it affect the great Breath at all?
>
> No, it does not affect the great Breath, except as a shadow which is reflected in the divine Sun and mirrored upon every existing being. For instance, when one person dies, every soul in the world feels it, some consciously and most unconsciously, in accordance with their closeness or distance to that particular soul. So the smallest cloud that crosses the face of the sun will darken the whole landscape and

throw a shadow over all things, great or small; but it does not rob the divine Spirit of Its power and wisdom.

So the destruction of the forms does not affect the great Breath at all, as the ebb and flow of the sea is not affected by the waves, whether the wave goes this way or that; but all through manifestation the manner of manifestation is the same, from the beginning to the end, and from God to the smallest atom. For instance, as God breathes, so we breathe, and so do the animals and birds[9]. Now the scientist has brought the proof that the trees breathe; as in its ebb and flow the sea breathes. When one sees this contraction and expansion going on in the whole universe in the same manner as it has begun, then one sees that in the whole creation – with its various aspects and all the differences there are in the nature and character of things and beings – there is one law and one manner in which the whole creation takes place and goes on to its finish.

Can you explain more why God inhales and exhales?

If God did not, the world could not exist. The condition of existence is inhaling and exhaling, and so God exists also. Only, His inhaling is the end of the whole creation. We say that this is a harm done to us, but is it unfair if we breathe? It may be unfair to many little germs whose lives are destroyed while we are breathing. Also there are lives that are created by our breathing. There will come a time when science will find out that the breath of man is creative, not only of atmosphere, but also of life; every atom created by the breath is a living being. At the root of this secret one will find out the reason for all disease.

Breath, as a living being, is creative. Science now finds out that behind every disease there is a germ of disease. There will come a time when one will find out that all disease comes from inhaling and exhaling.

As God creates and absorbs, so man creates and absorbs by his breath.

What difference is there between what God inhales and exhales?

The difference is in the character, the nature. His exhaling is creative, His inhaling is destroying. In Hindu terms: His inhaling is *Shiva*, His exhaling is *Brahma*.[10]

Is the destruction at the end of the inhaling sudden or gradual?

Gradual, just as we inhale and exhale gradually. At the finishing of the breath the destruction is finished. A picture of this is to be seen in the life of very large cobras. There are stories of people having seen very large cobras, in whose mouth even a cow or a buffalo could enter. Once in six months or a year, when they are hungry, they only have to open their mouth and, as they inhale, a cow is attracted and goes into their mouth. Then the cobra eats it and sleeps for six months or a year. This is a legend or a story, but I myself have noticed a large cobra eating a solid chicken, whole, not in parts, all at once!

The power of the cobra is great, because it is meditative. In mystical symbols the cobra has been made a mystical sign, because there is so much that one can learn from its life. It fasts for a long time, it goes without food, because it takes time to assimilate. It is not as greedy as a dog, it does not run after its food, it attracts food. The patience of the cobra is wonderful. It is this picture, therefore, that the mystics in their ancient mysticism have used as a symbol: the whole manifestation is attracted to the divine Spirit.

When the serpent has the tail in its mouth, it means perfection. Man and God are the two ends of the line. In the Qur'an it is said: 'All has come from God and to Him all will return.'

You named contraction and inhalation together,

but physically spoken inhalation is expansion.

The effect of inhaling has an effect upon the heart to expand, and when one exhales the effect is to contract. But really speaking the effect is the outcome, it is not the action. It is the action of contraction which produces inhaling of the breath, and it is the expansion which produces the contrary. We see this tendency in all beings.

We exhale what we inhale. If we inhale and were to keep ourselves in a better condition, our exhaling would become a healing.

If a person wants to take revenge, wants to harm another, then when he inhales his breath becomes poison, and when he exhales he does harm, because in his breath he has created numberless germs of illness which will disturb his own life and the life of those who come into his atmosphere.

Also, think of those who are inclined to kindness and love and sympathy, who have aspiration to goodness and have good thoughts. Their inhaling and exhaling will be uplifting and healing. Wherever their vibrations are moving will be their healing atmosphere.

Breath is not only physical, it touches the deepest part of our being. What we know is only inhaling and exhaling, what we feel through the nostrils. That is not breath. Breath is that power which makes us live, and which connects our body with our mind, our mind with our soul, and our soul with God.

Breath, in point of fact, is a rosary.

Is there a relation between breath and the soul?

Someone asked the Prophet[11] the meaning of the soul and the Prophet said: 'An act of God, an activity of Breath'. If I were to give an interpretation to this, I would say: 'An action of life, a movement of life. When life moved it turned into Breath'.

But if I were to say in my words what this creation is, I would also say: 'It is the Breath of God'. And if one asked: 'What is the end of it?' I would say: 'Only the indrawing of Breath'.

Nothing is lost, it is only inhaling and exhaling. The creation and what is called the annihilation or end – it is only the Breath of God.

CHAPTER 2

11th August, 1923, 5.30 p.m.

THE soul which is the ray of the divine Sun, in one sphere – the sphere in which it does not touch any earthly being – is called *malak*, or angel. Every soul passes through the angelic heavens; in other words, every soul is an angel before it touches the earthly plane. It is the angels who become human beings; those who do not become human beings remain angels. The human being, therefore, is a grown-up angel, and the angel is a soul who has not grown up. Infants who come on earth with their angelic qualities, and sometimes pass away without having experienced the life of the grown-up man, show us the picture of the original condition of the soul.

The idea that the angels are nearer to God is right according to this doctrine. Souls which have not journeyed farther are naturally close to the divine Spirit, they are angels. Someone asked the Prophet[11] why man was greater than the angels, man who causes all the bloodshed on the earth, while the angels are always occupied in the praise of God. The answer was that the angels knew nothing of the earth, they knew God, and so they occupied themselves with God. But man is greater, for when he comes on earth he has much in the world to be occupied with, and he still pursues God.

That angelic sphere is pure from passions and emotions, which are the source of all wrong and sin. Souls pure of all greed and desires given by the denseness of the earth are angels who know nothing else but happiness, for happiness is the real nature of the soul. The Hindus call the angels *suras*. *Sura* also means breath, and breath means life. *Suras*, therefore, mean pure lives, lives that live long. In the Hindu Scriptures there is another word used: *asura*, meaning lifeless, in other words, not in tune with the infinite.

THE SOUL TOWARDS MANIFESTATION

Man may continue to retain the angelic quality even in his life on earth as a human being, and it is the angelic quality which can be traced in some souls who show innocence and simplicity in their lives. This is not necessarily weakness or foolishness, it only shows the delicacy of a flower in the personality, together with fragrance. Angelic souls on the earth plane are inclined to love, to be kind, to be dependent upon those who show them love. They are ready to believe, willing to learn, inclined to follow that which seems to them for the moment good, beautiful and true. The picture of the angels that we read of in the Scriptures as sitting on clouds and playing harps, is but an expression of a mystical secret. Playing the harp is vibrating harmoniously. The angels have no actual harps, they themselves are the harps, they are living vibrations, they are life itself.

One can see in a person who is vibrating harmoniously that his presence becomes the inspiration of music and poetry. The person whose heart is tuned to the pitch of the angelic heavens will show on earth heavenly bliss. Therefore the wise seek the association of spiritual beings. Sitting on clouds means that the angels are above all clouds; clouds are for the beings of the dense earth. The angels are free from the momentary pleasures and the continuous spells of depression. Clouds do not touch them, for they are above clouds. Such souls who are in direct touch with the Spirit of God and who have no knowledge of the false world which is full of illusion, who live and know not death, whose lives are happiness, whose food is divine light, make around 'Arsh[12], the divine Spirit, an aura which is called the highest heaven.

Have the angels no relation to human life?
They have that of a child to a grown-up person.

In how far do angels help human beings?
As far as an infant can help a grown-up person.

What about the angels who remain angels?
They are in the highest glory.

What causes some to remain angels, and others to become human beings?

21

It is the strength with which the mechanism was wound, as is the nature of the clock. One clock goes on for the whole month, and the other clock wants a winding after twenty-four hours. There is another clock which can go on for a whole year. So is the mechanism of the whole life. There are some beings, some souls, which can go on much longer, because the winding is stronger; some less far, because the force behind them is not so strong.

It does not mean that the angels were meant to be angels and not to go farther, but it happens that the soul, which goes so far only, remains in that heaven. There are other souls which have greater power to go farther. They have gone through the angelic heavens and the sphere of the *djinn* and go farther still. It is the power by which they first started that gives the impetus. It is like the hoop of a child: it can go ten or more circles according to the striking of the stick. That striking is the work of God, the inner working of the divine Spirit.

What gives them the start?

If it is natural for a little child that his hoop, every time he strikes it, will not go as far as it went the first time, so it is that natural movement, which comes from the divine Spirit, that causes one to go farther than another.

Do those who remain angels return straight to God?

Yes, the return of the angel is straight to God; the return of the ray is straight to the flame from whence it came. If we study the light and the flames, we shall find that all the rays do not go evenly. Some go very far, others remain very near the flame. Every ray, large or small, has a different distance to which it reaches. So the short ray of the angels means that they have not reached as far as the dense earth.

What causes some beings to become mortal and some to remain angels?

It is the mortal garb that they take, and therefore it is

the garb which is mortal. They are not mortal but mortality is impressed upon the consciousness of the soul; it is the garb that the soul has adopted for its use. So every person begins by thinking: 'I am my body', and from that time the illness of the body makes him think: 'I am ill', and the death of the body means: 'I am dead' to that person. Then he becomes his garb, he is not himself. If there is any illusion, it is this.

Are all souls angels from the beginning of their journey towards manifestation?

Yes, since all has come from God, then all has come from the divine Light, and the first offshoot of the divine Light is the angel.

Do they experience life on each succeeding plane of existence, going towards physical life?

Yes, they do, but not all. For instance, imagine a picture of a thousand birds starting from Paris to go to England. Some were able to go as far as Rouen; there they liked the place, they stayed there, they enjoyed it, they forgot all about England. Some went to Le Havre and they enjoyed the sea shore and just lived there and were happy. Some went still farther, crossed the Channel and arrived in England. Those who stayed in Rouen had not a very long journey to come back to Paris again, but those who had crossed, for them it was a very long journey to come back.

Do angels have a form?

This is a question which is very subtle and most difficult to explain in words. The reason is that every thing or being that has a name, has a form, but we are accustomed only to call something which we can see a form, and what our eyes cannot see – we do not call it a form. To conceive the form of an angel, we must become an angel: we must turn into an angel to conceive what the true angelic form is. We are accustomed to picture every form like our own, therefore whenever we think of fairies or angels, spirits or ghosts, we picture them like us. The fairies of the Chinese have Chinese features and the fairies of the Russians have Russian hats, because the mind pictures what it is accustomed to see.

What form have angels when they appear in a vision?

The vision itself will cover them under that form in which man is accustomed to see them. The form we imagine covers the angelic form.

What is the meaning of the angels who, in the stories of the Old Testament, appeared to man? Were they real apparitions?

That angel is called *farishta*, one who is sent. They are real to the extent to which they are intelligible to those to whom they are sent.

Are souls on their return from the physical plane also called angels?

No, they are called spirits.

Does the soul on its return also go through the angelic sphere?

Yes, it does. In that case there are different names for that soul. Souls on their return journey pass through the angelic plane as spirits and may remain there a long time.

What is the opposite of the angels? What are those which are by some called evil spirits? Are they fallen angels?

If the angel fell, it would not be an angel, for it would fall on the earth and as soon as it touched the earth, it would not be an angel any longer!

'Evil spirit' is quite a different thing. It is a word applied to a soul which has passed from the earth and which has collected all the evil through life.

Would you tell us something of the *asuras* whose life is caught in the net of mortality?[13]

Asuras are those who have lost their souls. In answer

to the question: how one can lose one's soul which is the very life, and still live, I do not mean to say that the soul left them, but that they lost consciousness of their soul. When one is not conscious of his soul, his spirit has lost it; at least, the soul is lost from his consciousness.

It is just like the person who had buried a large sum of money in the ground of his farm and who then went to another country. Somebody came who said: 'All the money has been taken away.' This person became very unhappy. Now, really speaking, the other one did not tell the truth. This person still has his money where it lies buried, but just now he is conscious of the loss; so for the moment he has lost it. When he goes and digs it up, he will find that it is there; but for the moment, till he has dug it up, it is lost. So the soul is not lost in reality, but for the sake of convenience we say: the soul is lost.

CHAPTER 3

13th August, 1923, 5.30 p.m.

THE souls in the angelic heavens have all goodness, and this shows that goodness is natural; and what is contrary to our nature we call evil. The souls in the angelic heavens are innocent; this also shows that innocence is the natural condition of the soul, and the lack of innocence is a foreign element which the soul acquires after coming upon earth. In the angelic spheres the souls are happy; this shows that unhappiness does not belong to the soul, it is something which is foreign to it. Therefore in the experience of man the discomfort coming out of life gives unhappiness.

The souls on the earth have something of the angelic quality: they readily respond and are attracted without resistance to the innocence, happiness and goodness of another person. If they knew that it is because this is the original quality of the soul, they would develop the same in their own being. As Rumi said: 'People are drawn towards me and they shed tears with

25

my cry, and yet they know not what it is in me that attracts them.'[14] Seeking after goodness, innocence and happiness helps the angelic qualities to develop in a soul. Spirituality, therefore, is the development of the angelic quality, and love of spirituality is the longing for the angelic heavens, it is homesickness.

Does death frighten the spiritual being? No, death for the spiritual soul is only a gate through which it enters into that sphere which every soul knows to be its home. Souls who become conscious of the angelic heavens, even in the smallest degree, hear the call of that sphere, and if they have any discomfort in this world, it is that of the homesickness which the call of the angelic heavens gives.

The soul may be likened to a ray of the sun. So the angels, not being adorned with physical garbs, are lights, are flames themselves. The Scriptures therefore say that the angels are made of *Nūr*, or Light. *Nūr* is specially that Light which comes from the divine Sun, the Spirit of God. All souls are made of that essence, which is the essence of the whole manifestation. In every soul there exists some part of that essence, however little. The quality of that essence is that it absorbs all that is around it and in time develops, so that it will merge into its own element which is divine.

If the soul coming on earth is an angel and is affected by the returning spirits, why are not all the angels affected by those spirits?

A sphere means a certain limit, a certain horizon. It means that in that horizon nothing dense or earthly can enter; before it enters it must be melted. Therefore the souls in those spheres are not touched by any souls coming from the earth. No souls coming from the earth are allowed to enter those spheres before they are purified from all elements of denseness. As an example very well known in India there is the story of Indra. It is a story that has been made into dramas and operas and has been produced for ages. The people of India have never tired of it; for them it is always new, always interesting, because it has an interest both for the ordinary mind and for the thinking mind.

THE SOUL TOWARDS MANIFESTATION

The story is that a prince was taken up into heaven by a fairy who loved him, and the prince urged on the fairy to take him to the court of Indra, where she was appointed to dance every day. The fairy refused, 'because', as she said, 'no earthly being is allowed to enter heaven. I have already done something against the rule; to bring you now to the court of Indra will be the end of your life'.

The prince said: 'I will not listen, I must see where you go.'

After a time she said: 'If you wish it, I will take you.'

She took him to the court of Indra where she was appointed to dance, and she told him to hide behind her wings. But the wings could not cover him, and those who saw him told Indra that a man from the dense earth, who was not allowed to come to heaven, was brought there by the fairy. The wrath of Indra arose and he said: 'I will cast him down with the fairy who was privileged to be in heaven. She shall live a life in the wilderness, a life of loneliness for many years to come. Until she is purified of the five elements she will not be able to enter the spheres of heaven, and for this man there will be another sphere of wilderness.'

It is an allegorical story; the fairy is the soul, and the man is the body. They were separated because in heaven there is no place for both body and soul. The place of the body is only on the earth, and however much the soul tried to take the body to heaven, there was no place for it there. The soul was also cast out because it loved the body too much. When they were purified of the five elements they were no longer of fire, earth, water, air and ether. Then only the angel remained. When the human has gone away, what remains? The angel only.[15]

The soul that goes back, does it go back rich? Does it develop spiritually?

It is spiritual already.

Why has it come?

To get the experience of the earthly spheres.

And then to lose it?,

Yes, it finds nothing in it.

Why is there less of the essence of the Spirit of God in one soul than in another? Do we not all come on earth with the same quantity of that essence?

No, God is not so inartistic as to make all alike. Even on the tree every fruit is different, every flower on the same plant is different. If there were no differences there would be no joy in life. Life is interesting because of differences.

Then a soul which has less to begin with is handicapped!

No one is handicapped in life, for life is progressive. Some have more to begin with and less in the end.

When one is purged of the five elements, are all the souls equal then?

There is variation still. Where there is duality there is variation. Where there are two flames they are not alike. In truth there is one, but in fact there are two; when there are two, there are many, and not two the same.

If the soul keeps its angelic qualities on earth and does not experience earthly passion and experiences, why does it come on earth? Is it only to be an example for others?

If you think so, yes. No one lives without action and every action has its meaning. So no one has come here without a purpose. If we cannot understand the meaning of his life and action, it does not mean that that person has not come on earth for a purpose. Therefore in the sum total of the whole working of the universe every individual seems to have filled a certain place which was meant for him, and has been of a certain use in the working of the whole scheme of the universe. No one in this world is useless.

A person who sits in the midst of the crowd and is busy the whole day, and another person who has gone in the wilderness, whom no one sees, they are all busy, even the latter. The most occupied and the most lazy, the most useful and the most useless, they all have their part to perform in this drama of life. Only the difference between the wise and everybody is, that everybody does not know the secret, the meaning of life, while the wise gains wisdom in learning to understand the meaning of life.

CHAPTER 4

14th August, 1923, 5.30 p.m.

THE soul going forth towards manifestation, which is still in the angelic heavens, is free from all the differences and distinctions which are the conditions of the soul's life on earth.

Are angels male and female? The dual aspect starts even from the angelic heavens. God alone is above duality. In all other conditions and aspects of life this duality is to be seen, though it is more distinct on the earth plane. In the angelic heavens it is not distinguishable.

People often ask if the angels are in touch with people on earth. The answer is that their life does not necessitate any communication with human life on earth, except in the case of some who are destined to perform a certain duty on earth. It is mentioned in the ancient Scriptures that angels came with messages to the prophets of Beni Israël. The explanation of this from the metaphysical point of view is quite different from what an ordinary person would imagine. No man on earth is capable of communicating with the angels in heaven, nor is an angel from heaven inclined to communicate with man. But in the exceptional lives of the prophets what happens is that they rise above all the planes which keep man removed from the angelic heavens, and by doing so they are able to touch these heavens. Being charged with the ever glowing fire of inspiration from the angelic spheres where they come into touch with the angels, they descend to the plane of the earth and it is then that their words become tongues of flame, as spoken of in the Scriptures. This means that every word of theirs becomes a torch in the hands of those who listen, to illuminate their path through life. Especially is this so in the lives of the great ones, who have given a divine Message, a religion, to the world. Their souls have never been disconnected in any way from the angelic world; it is this current, which linked their souls with the souls of the angels, that always kept them in contact with both heaven and earth. The soul of the prophet, therefore, is a link between heaven and earth; it is a medium by which God's Message can be received.

Then there are some spiritual souls who have had the experience in their lives of having been warned or helped by an angel. It is such souls who have kept a thread unbroken which they brought with them from the angelic world. They may be conscious of it or not, but there is a telegraphic wire which connects their souls with the souls of the angels, and they are conscious of having had contact with angels. Common disease is called normal health. When many cannot experience something which is rare, they think the person who can experience such a thing has gone mad. Therefore it is the law of the mystics to see all things, to experience all things, both of heaven and earth, and yet to say little, for the souls incapable of understanding the possibility of their reach will ridicule them.

There is another aspect of the contact with the angels, and that is at the time of death. Many have seen in their lives the Angels of Death at the time when death's call comes. Some have seen them in human form, some have not seen them but have heard them speak. The reason is that there are some souls who have already departed from the earth plane, though the breath is still there connecting the soul with the body. Such souls experience, while still on the earth, the angelic spheres at the time of their death. They see angels garbed in the form of their own imagination and hear the words of the angels in their own language. The reason is that it is necessary for a person who has lived on the earthly plane to clothe a being of the higher planes in earthly garments, and to interpret immediately the language of the higher spheres in his own words. For instance, the angel Gabriel spoke to Moses in the Hebrew language, and to Mohammed in Arabic. One might ask, which was the language of the angel Gabriel, Arabic or Hebrew? Neither Arabic nor Hebrew was the language of Gabriel. His language was the language of the soul, and the soul knows the language of the soul. It is when a person interprets what he hears, even to himself, that he clothes the words he hears in his own language.

When it is said that the Spirit descended upon the twelve apostles and they began to speak all languages, the meaning is that when they were inspired by the angelic world, by the divine Sun, or the Holy Ghost, they knew the language of all languages, for it was the language of the soul. This means that they heard the voice of the soul before men spoke to them in earthly words; they were able to hear the voice of every soul through that inspiration. It would not be giving any special credit to the apostles if one said they knew all languages in the world instantaneously, for there are people even now to be found whose genius as linguists is so great that they know more than twenty or thirty languages. (And even then they do not know all languages!) There is only one language which may be called 'all languages' and that is the language of the soul.

Before the illuminated soul all souls stand as written letters.

What did you say: the Holy Ghost is the divine Son or the divine Sun?

I meant both.

What is the imagination about the Angel of Death? Is it something unreal?

The imagination is everything. To the real all is real, to the unreal all is unreal.

Has it nothing to do with spiritual truth?

Nothing.

What is it then?

The angels are purely souls.

What part of the soul is imagination?

It is not part of the soul, it is part of the mind. Imagination is the work of the mind.

31

How can we know that is the Angel of Death we see, if we clothe it with our imagination?

But what is our imagination? Very often our imagination is inspiration, intuition. Especially at the time of death a person is pitched to a very high state of being. So even if he had not much inspiration during his life-time, he has it then, for then he is lifted up already – before the breath has left the body – closer to the higher spheres. Therefore, though he clothes the angels with his imagination, still his intuition tells him that it is the Angel of Death.

Is there one Angel of Death, or more?

There is one, and there are many. And yet in many there is one, and in one there are many.

Why does the Roman Catholic Church divide the angels into nine grades, the Seraphins nearest to God, the Archangels nearest to man?

Variety always exists. Where there is a number of entities, there will be variety and in variety difference. It is quite true that we find the same among the dwellers on earth. Some are attracted to the earth, some to heaven. So among angels there is also the same tendency. Some are attracted to those who have travelled farther – that is man –, others are content to remain in their own sphere and to enjoy the heavenly bliss.

Do you think that scientific or inventive genius stands in the same relationship to the angelic spheres as prophetic genius?

Yes, certainly, although prophetic genius is all embracing. Scientific and inventive genius has the same source of inspiration, and all that depends on inspiration has much to do with the angelic spheres.

In what way are angels, *dēvas* and spirits different?

Angels inhabit the angelic spheres.

Dēvas are among men such as *Walī, Ghawth, Quṭb, Nabī, Rasūl*[16], who have come to the earth, and yet are as a fruit dropped on the earth but still connected with the branch. The branch has bent and the fruit has touched the earth, but it has not lost connection with the stem. It is that soul which is called *dēva*.

Nature spirits, like human beings, have souls and so have the birds and beasts and insects. Not only these living creatures, but also trees and plants, planets and stars, everything that exists has spirit at the back of it, and this spirit is its soul.

Can you tell me, if a soul who has passed away young and has been a pure soul on earth, helps more in a higher plane than it would have done on earth?

Every soul inclined to help has a scope in every plane, on this plane as well as on the higher planes. He who is able to help in this plane, is able to help in the higher plane even more. A pure soul can help here, and in the higher plane even more.

Can we help somebody more as a human being, or on a higher plane?

In some ways and in some things one can help more as a human being, and in some other ways one can help more without a body, for there are the limitations of the human body which cannot arrive in a certain place earlier than in due time. But once passed from this plane one can get sooner wherever one wants to go. The one who is living in the physical body has many facilities also, for when a person is face to face with a friend, he can help that friend much more than being hidden from the sight of the friend who does not see him.

Please tell us about guardian angels.

Guardian angels are nothing but extra light on the path. There is one's own light and the light one is seeking from above. He who holds himself closer to heaven, has a guidance from heaven, he is always guarded. He who disconnects himself from his original abode which is heaven, becomes worldly, earthly. He is as a fruit broken from the tree and fallen on the earth. But he who still clings to the light of heaven has a light with him, about him, to guide him, and at every step that light comes, warns him, guides him, in accordance with his desire for guidance.

CHAPTER 5

15th August, 1923, 5.30 p.m.

THE guardian angel is a term known to many. This angelic protection comes to some souls on earth, such souls as are walking on the earth and yet are linked in some way or other with the heavenly spheres. Often one sees an innocent child being saved from an accident and often a person is warned to save a child at the moment when it is in danger. This guardian angel also appears in the same form as the angels sent to people on different duties.

There are recording angels, who take a record of our good and bad actions, and the most interesting thing is that those who keep the record of the good actions do not keep the record of the bad actions. Those who keep a record of the bad actions are other angels. There is a further explanation given by the Prophet on this subject: that often a discussion takes place between those who keep the record of the good deeds and those who record the evil deeds. The former do not believe in the latter, because they are only conscious of man's goodness; they cannot believe that one who is good, can be bad as well. Also those who record the good points want their record to be filled, and the other angels want their record to be filled. So there is a great rivalry between them. Is this not the condition we see in human nature? There is no person living on earth of whom all say good things and no one says bad things. And there is no person living about whom all say bad things and no one says any good. The most interesting point for a keen observer of life is how each tries to prove his argument to be correct. In Sufi terms these two are called the angels of *Khayr* and *Khār*; the difference in the spelling is very small. This suggests how little the difference is between goodness and badness. As Omar Khayyam says:

THE SOUL TOWARDS MANIFESTATION

A hair divides perhaps the false and true,
Yes, and a single *alif* were the clue –
Could you but find it – to the treasure house
And, peradventure, to the Master too.

The ancient belief is that immediately after a dead person is buried these two parties of angels come to his grave with their records and dispute about him. But do we not see in human nature the same thing? People do not even wait until after death; they begin to say good and bad things about the person they know, about their friends and foes, and dispute about them even during their life-time.

There is also an ancient belief that after the dead person is put into his grave and buried, two angels come to ask him questions and by this cross-examination prove their arguments for and against. Their names are *Munkir* and *Nākir*. I think there is very little difference in their names.[17]

There is a story in the Bible that Jacob wrestled with an angel all night and before the breaking of the dawn Jacob won. The angel asked him his name, blessed him and gave him a new name. The interpretation of this is that the illuminated souls of the angels coming into contact with earthly beings are in conflict. That conflict ends when man has given up his earthly point of view and adopts the heavenly point of view. Then there is no more conflict, but a blessing. The asking of the name is a paradox, for once the false ego is crushed the soul does not know what its real name is: the name belongs to the false ego.

There is an old conception of nine kinds of angels. In reality there is only one kind of angels, but their relation with human beings and their desire to experience life through human beings divides them into nine kinds.

Then there is a belief that there are angels who are the inhabitants of heaven and others who live in the contrary place. Those of heaven are called the angels of *nūr*, and the others angels of *nār*. This is an extreme point of view. In reality they can be distinguished as two kinds: angels of *jalāl*[18] and angels of *jamāl*, angels of power and angels of beauty.

A question arises as to why the angels, who descend on earth as angels, do not come as human beings, for every human being was originally an angel. The answer is that the angels who are related with human beings are human souls now in the angelic world, who keep connection with human beings because of their wish; they have returned from the earthly regions to the angelic heavens, and they still keep in touch with the earth either for a certain duty or for their own pleasure.

The great angels of whom we read in the Scriptures, such as Gabriel, were they ever in human form?

Gabriel is the chief angel of inspiration, of the prophetic Message, of revelation, and so this is the central ray, the ray of the prophets, of the Messengers, the inspirer of the great beings of the world. Therefore Gabriel belongs to his own kind.

Why are there nine kinds of angels?

Because they are delighted in nine things.

Are the recording angels symbolical?

Why symbolical when their existence is a separate existence? They exist, they are angels. What is on earth is in heaven; the nature and character of the earth is also in heaven. If human nature has a tendency, in heaven they show the same tendency; and as men are concerned with the good and evil of one another, so are the angels.

Was it symbolical that they came to the grave and disputed over it?

Yes, that is to some extent symbolical.

Do angels who have descended on earth take interest in human affairs?

No. Angels are not interested in the same way as human beings, because there is a great gap between them, their interests are not the same. Therefore if ever angels come on the earth, they are either in touch with the innocent souls of children, because they are closer to their sphere, or they are interested in the illuminated soul, the spiritual soul. They are also interested in the being who is passing away from the earth and going to their country.

As the recording angels write down the good and

bad actions, there must be a judge.

The judge is in man's heart. It is from man's heart that the angels read what they have to note as his good and his bad actions.

As man is judged by the God in his own heart, what is the use of this outside recording of our actions by the angels?

But it all goes on in the plane of our heart! God, the angelic world, the universe, all is in the heart. We are accustomed to put it outside, but it is all in our heart. It is not outside at all.

What is the heart?

The heart is a mirror which has two sides. It reflects all that is outside and all that is within. Therefore God and angels and all that is within, is reflected in the heart. All that is outside is also reflected, because the mirror has two sides.

The heart is not necessarily a piece of flesh. The heart of flesh is only that organ in the body which was made first and upon which the whole body was formed. Therefore, as it was made first, it is more sensitive to the heart which is within than any other organ, and so when there is depression, joy, or pleasure, any little excitement or little feeling, it produces a feeling in the heart. As man does not see the real heart which is a mirror of heaven and earth, he calls that piece of flesh, where is the seat of the function, the heart.

The soul is incomparably greater than the body, yet man thinks that the soul is hidden somewhere in the body – he does not know where. Therefore man gives great importance to his body.

Please explain how the heart of man is the heart of the universe.

In the heart of man the whole universe is reflected, and as the whole universe is reflected in the heart of man it may be called the heart of the universe.

What is the heart and what is the soul?

Suppose we take a lamp, a burning lamp, as a picture of the human being. The flame is the soul and the globe is the heart. The inner part of the globe is the heart, the outer part is the mind, and the shade over the lamp is the body.

CHAPTER 6

17th August, 1923, 5.30 p.m.

THE angelic spheres, the highest heavens, are the spheres of Light which is called *Nūr*; and that current of power which runs through the divine Sun causes rays to spread, each ray being an angel or a soul. It is this divine current which really speaking is *nafs*[19], which means breath or the ego. Breath is the ego and ego is the breath. When the breath has left the body, the ego has gone. The nature of this current, which spreads as a ray and which is a life-current, is to collect and to create. It collects the atoms of the sphere through which it is running, and it creates out of itself all that it can create. Therefore in the angelic heaven, which is the sphere of radiance, the soul collects the atoms of radiance. A Sufi poet of Persia has given a most beautiful expression of this idea in a verse: 'A glow came garbed in a flame'. No better picture of an angel can one make than this. Before the angels were drawn by artists in the form of human beings, they were symbolized as burning lamps. From this comes the custom of lighting candles in religious services, thereby showing, to some extent, what the angels were like before they became human souls.

In the ancient Scriptures it is mentioned that human beings produced angels by their virtues; but this is only a symbolical expression. It is not that human beings produced angels by their virtues, but that their virtues lifted their souls to the angels, and connected them with the angels.

One may ask: if the souls who have settled in the angelic heaven are angels, then what makes them come to the earth? How can they experience life on earth? The answer is that it is not the angels who have settled in the angelic heaven who come to the earth, for these rays have finished their creative power in manifesting as angels. If they had had a greater power they would certainly have gone farther, even to the physical plane, and would preferably have manifested as human beings, for the desire of every soul is to reach the ultimate culmination in manifestation, and that culmination is the stage of the human plane. [20]

It is the work of the souls who return from the earth to communicate with the earth very often, and it is such angels who are generally known to man. Angels who have never manifested as men on earth – if they ever do experience life on the earth – only experience it by the medium of minds and bodies which, by their evolution, come closer to the angelic heaven. They take these as their instruments, and at times reflect themselves in them and at times have them reflected in themselves.

> If *nafs* exist as far back as the angelic heavens, how can human beings hope to become free from it?
>
> Human beings do not need to be free from it, but they need to distinguish between the true *nafs* and the false.
>
> When angels experience life on the earth through the minds and bodies of human beings, is this obsession and should it be avoided?
>
> Certainly it is obsession, but at the same time, in the case of the angel it is not necessary to avoid it, because from there one gets nothing but Light. All inspiration comes from the angelic sphere.
>
> Would one be very fortunate to get it?
>
> Yes, I should think so.
>
> Do you mean to say that angels who have not manifested obsess human beings?
>
> Yes, it is so.
>
> Could you use a more beautiful word, because obsession is connected with less good things. Perhaps inspired?
>
> Yes, inspired.

When the force emanates from the divine source, it projects rays going towards manifestation. Does each ray spread in all directions?

Yes, the nature of the rays is the same in the divine sphere as in the physical sphere. We see this by studying the rays of the sun.

Is the soul centred where the physical body is?

It is in the body in one way. It functions in the body, although the soul is incomparably larger than the body. Just a little point of the soul functions in the body, but its size is much larger. The impression one has, is that the soul is centred in the body, when as a matter of fact it extends throughout the universe.[21]

Are there any distinctions or differences of race, nationality or religion among the souls who have passed from the physical plane?

The differences and distinctions still remain. It is not so very easy to get rid of them. Wherever there is a world of variety there are differences. Yes, one can say that in the higher plane there are fewer distinctions, in the lower plane there are more. Even among human beings we find: the more evolved, the fewer distinctions, and the less evolved, the more distinctions.

Do the angels of the angelic heavens also experience birth and death, youth and old age?

Not in the sense we are accustomed to understand, but at the same time there is only one being – God – Who is above birth and death. All else, all manifestation, from the point of duality to the myriads of beings, all are subject to the law of birth and death. Only the difference in birth and death on the plane of human beings and on the plane of angels is very great; but youth and age are in everything we see. For the plants and fruits there is a time when they are raw and a time when they are ripe; and so it is with the angels. But there is no comparison between the life of the angels and the life of human beings. Human life on earth is too limited to be compared with the life of the angels.

Even the time between the birth and death of a thought, an idea, is incomparably small when compared to the life of angels.

Can every atom of the manifestation be said to have a soul?

Certainly, because manifestation commenced from the heavenly source, from the divine spheres. Therefore every atom of this universe, mental or material, is an outcome of that source and cannot exist without having a part of that heavenly radiance within it. Even a mote of dust has a radiance behind it and if it were not for this radiance it would not have manifested to our view. We see it because it has light in it; it is its own light that shows it to us. That is its soul.

What seems to be void of Intelligence is not in reality void of it, only the Intelligence is buried in its heart. It is, so to speak, Intelligence that has projected itself, and then its own outcome has covered it and buried the Intelligence in itself; but the Intelligence must come out some day. Therefore, through all these phases of life it is trying to break out. You can see this in volcanic eruptions. This power is working in floods, lightning, stars and planets. Its desire is to burst out when it is in a way captive, and its chance of rising is in human life. For that reason spirituality is the only object of fulfilment in human evolution.

Is that what is meant in the expression: the spiritual realization of matter?

Yes.

CHAPTER 7

18th August, 1923, 5.30 p.m.

SOULS in the angelic heavens live as a breath. The soul in its nature is a current; the nature of this current is to envelop in itself all that may come along and meet it on its way[22]. The soul collects all that comes to it. Therefore it becomes different from its original condition. Yet in its real being the soul is a vibration, the soul is a breath, the soul is the Essence, the soul is Intelligence, and the soul is the essence of the personality.

The question very often arises: if an angel comes from above, does it descend outwardly before a person, or manifest within a person in his heart? The lift for the soul, which brings it down on earth and takes it back to heaven, is situated within, not without. That lift is the breath. The soul comes to earth with the breath, and with the breath it returns. Those among human beings who are not even aware of their own breath, how can they know who comes within themselves and who goes out? Many seem wide awake to the life without, but asleep to the life within; though the chamber of their heart is continually visited by the hosts of heaven, they do not know their heart, they are not there.

There is a very interesting story told in the Arabic Scriptures. It is that God made Iblis the chief among all angels and then told him to bring some clay that he might make out of it an image. The angels, under the direction of Iblis, brought the clay and he made an image. Then God breathed into that image and asked the angels to bow before it. All the angels bowed but Iblis. He said: 'Lord, Thou hast made me the chief of all angels, and I have brought this clay at Thy command and made with my own hands this image which Thou commandest me to bow before!' The displeasure of God arose and fell on his neck as the sign of the outcast.

This story helps us to understand what Jesus Christ meant when he said: 'Blessed are the meek, for they shall inherit the earth'. What Iblis denied, was the reflection of God in man. One can observe the same law in every direction of life: a person may be rich in wealth or high in position, but he must still obey the policeman. It is not the rank or wealth which the latter has, but the power of the government which is reflected in him, and when a man takes no heed of the policeman, he refuses to obey the law of the State. In everything, small or great, it is the same law; and in every person there is a spark of this tendency of Iblis, the tendency which we know as egotism, the tendency to say: 'No, I will not listen, I will not give in, I will not consider'. Because of what? Because of 'I', because of 'I am'. But there is only one 'I', the perfect 'I', Who is God, Whose power is mightier than any power existing in the world, Whose position is greater than that of anyone; and He shows it in answer to the egotistic tendency of man, who is limited. This is expressed in the saying: man proposes but God disposes. It is this idea which teaches man the virtue of resignation, which shows him that the 'I' he claims is a much smaller 'I', and that there is no comparison between his 'I' and the 'I' of the great Ego God.

Another story tells how frightened the soul was when it was commanded to enter the body of clay. It was most unwilling, not from pride but from fear. The soul whose nature is freedom, whose dwelling-place is heaven, whose comfort it is to be free to dwell in all the spheres of existence – to have to dwell in a house made of clay was for that soul most horrifying. Then God asked the angels to play and sing and the ecstacy that was produced in the soul by hearing that music made it enter the body of clay, where it became captive to death.

The interpretation of this idea is that the soul, which is pure intelligence and angelic in its being, had not the least interest in dwelling in the physical plane, which robs it of its freedom and makes it limited: what interested the soul and made it come into the body is what this physical world offers to the senses. This produces such an intoxication that it takes away for the moment the thought of heaven from the soul, and so the soul becomes captive in the physical body.

What is Cupid? Is not Cupid the soul? It is the soul, it is the angel, the angel going towards manifestation, the angel which has arrived at its destination, the human plane. Before it manifests there, it is Cupid.[23]

You said that enjoyment through the senses made the soul willing to remain in the body. Does it get more enjoyment in the senses on earth, than it would without them in heaven?

No, I did not say that the enjoyment in the senses made the soul willing to *remain* in the body. I said that the enjoyment through the senses made the soul *come* into the body. It would not have entered otherwise, because through the senses the physical life became intelligible to the soul, and therefore it intoxicated the soul so that it entered the body.

One might ask: how did it experience the senses before entering the body? It experienced the senses through those of other mediums, of those who are in the body. As the child shares the food of the mother before its birth, so the soul experiences through the senses of others before its own senses have developed.

Then the desire is to have the senses for itself?

Yes.

The socialist point of view that all property is theft is an extreme attitude. Those who say this do not know that, if there was not this 'theft' as an inner impulse behind this manifestation, the souls would not have come on earth. What induces the soul to come on earth is the desire to approach near it, to take possession of it, to utilize it to its best advantage, and to guard against its being taken away. That is the nature of the soul. This is the difference between the socialistic point of view and the mystical idea. The socialist says: 'That is unjust', and he does not see that it is nature and natural. Without this, life would not have been possible.

Does it get more enjoyment on earth through the senses than it would without them in heaven?

The enjoyment that the soul gets here on earth through the medium of the senses is like wine which just touches the lips; it is an illusion, no wine. As the world is illusive, so enjoyment is the same. It has never made one happy nor will the senses ever make one happy for ever. The pleasures of the world come and go; for a moment they are pleasant, afterwards it is nothing.

There is only one pleasure which is real happiness. It does not belong to the earth. If a person who is living on the earth is happy there, he is not happy with earthly things, but only with the realization of heaven when he connects his soul with the heavenly spheres. In the things of the earth there is no happiness, only pleasure which is illusive.

Can he enjoy that happiness in worldly things?

A soul which is in the body, although connected with heaven, is still open to the influences of the earth; not only open but dependent for its external life on food, on earth, on water. As its outer life depends upon the things of the earth, it still seeks for the pleasures of the earth. The closer a person is drawn to heaven, the less important become the pleasures of the earth. All that seems to be pleasure fades away and has no colour, no taste any more.

Therefore religions have taught self-denial by denying all the pleasures of the earth, but I think a soul which naturally rises towards heaven does not need to practise this self-denial. It comes by itself, as the soul grows and rises towards heaven.

Was not the question why should a soul, which has not yet manifested, leave the greater happiness of heaven for earthly pleasures?

The idea is that the tendency of every motive is to go to the utmost point, to the farthest point, whether its result gives happiness or unhappiness. The tendency of the one who has a motive is to experience it to its final result. For instance, a singer sings. He sings very comfortably on the lower notes, but his heart's desire is to go as high as he can. He may take a chance of breaking his voice, but his tendency is to go the highest note. It is the same tendency which makes people go to the North Pole.

If their life was taken away, or at the cost of whatever suffering – yet they will go to the extreme end of the world.

If there was not this tendency in the soul, there would not have been manifestation. Even at the cost of all the happiness in heaven, the soul touches the utmost point. Manifestation in the human form is the utmost border of manifestation, the farthest one can go. Human evolution comes to that great fulfilment, with which even the angels are not blessed. Therefore there is advantage in every loss. There is a loss for the time being, but there is a greater benefit in the end.

Then this does mean that they are sent into manifestation, they cannot help it?

That is when we look at the whole universe automatically working; but when we come to the individual, there is a spark of freewill which starts from the angelic heavens.★

What does 'the sign of the outcast' mean, that Iblis received?

I have interpreted it as the sign of the outcast. In Arabic it is called *ṭawq*[24] which means that something was taken away from him that made him chief, that was the secret of evolution, of progress.

Plainly speaking, the soul who has not yet realized the almighty power of God and the perfect wisdom of God and who has not compared his own limited power and wisdom with the almighty power and wisdom of God, is in the same place where Iblis was. Every soul, to some extent, is Iblis. But the moment the soul compares his limitation to the perfection of God, he is already on the way of progress, because realizing and becoming conscious of his imperfection gives him the tendency to go forward to that perfection which is the perfection of God.

★See Appendix, page 183 on the Question if the Universe is going on automatically.

Is there the same idea in the tale of the angel Iblis and the angel Lucifer?

Yes.

Is fear inherent in the soul, as you said the angels feared the contact with the body?

Fear is a shadow cast upon the light of the soul. And of what is that shadow? That shadow is of something that the soul does not know, something that is strange to it. For instance, take a person near the water who has never learned to swim; he is not acquainted with water, he is not at ease, there is his fear. Another person gets rid of that feeling of strangeness, he knows his own power over the water, he has no more fear. Therefore, fear comes from ignorance. As everyone fears to go in a dark room when he does not know what is there, so the soul in entering the body of clay naturally is frightened.

In death, is it the fear of the soul, or of the physical body to be broken up?

Of the soul which does not know what death is. Death is the strangeness.*

CHAPTER 8

20th August, 1923 5.30 p.m.

THE soul which has passed through the angelic heavens comes next on to the sphere of the *djinn* or *genius*[25]. This is the sphere of mind and may be called the spiritual sphere, for it is mind and soul which make spirit. The souls which halt in this sphere, being attracted by its beauty, settle here. Also the souls which have no more power to go farther into outer manifestation become the inhabitants of this sphere. Therefore there are three kinds of souls which meet in this sphere on their way to manifestation: the souls which are attracted to this

*See Appendix page 184 on The Fear for Death.

sphere and which decide to remain here, the souls which are unable to go farther and which have to settle there, and the souls which are continuing their journey towards the earth plane and which are on their way to the earth through this plane.

The *djinn* is an entity with a mind, but not such a mind as that of man, a purer, clearer mind, which is illuminated by the Light of Intelligence. The mind of the *djinn* is deeper in perception and in conception, because it is empty – not filled with thoughts and imaginations as is that of man. It is the mind of the *djinn* which may be called the empty cup – a cup into which knowledge can be poured, in which there is accommodation. It is for this reason that the teachers on the spiritual path appreciate the *djinn* quality in the mind of their pupils in which they find accommodation for knowledge. A cup which is already filled, or even partially filled, does not give free accommodation for that knowledge which the teacher wishes to pour into the heart of his pupil. As the *djinns* are keen in perception and conception, so they are keen in expression either in word or deed. The action of the *djinn* extends as far as the mind can reach and the word of the *djinn* reaches even farther than the voice, for it takes as its route the mental sphere, which is above the air waves.

The *djinn* comes closer to man than the angel, for in the *djinn* there is something like the mind, which is completed in man. All the intuitive and inspirational properties are possessed by the *djinn*, because that is the only source that the *djinn* has of receiving its knowledge. Subjects such as poetry, music, art, inventive science, philosophy and morals are akin to the nature of the *djinn*. The artist, therefore, and the poet, also the musician and the philosopher show in their gifts the *djinn* heritage, which proves them throughout their lives to be geniuses.

The word *djinn* comes from a Sanskrit word *jnāna*, which means knowledge. The *djinns*, therefore, are the beings of knowledge, whose hunger is for knowledge, whose joy is in learning, in understanding, and whose work is in inspiring and bringing joy and light to others. In every kind of knowledge that exists the favourite knowledge to a *djinn* is the knowledge of truth, in which is the fulfilment of its life's purpose.

THE SOUL TOWARDS MANIFESTATION

Are there good and bad *djinns*?

Where there is good, there is bad. Good cannot exist without bad. If *djinns* are good, so *djinns* must be bad also.

Are there good and bad angels?

If there are good angels, then there are bad also. The question is only if they are good. They cannot be good, if there was no bad. The angels can only be good on the condition that some of them are bad.

Do souls remain a very long time in the angelic and *djinn*-plane on the return journey, as they do on their way towards manifestation?

Yes, certainly. Freewill is the basis of the whole life. In spite of all limitations and helplessness that man meets through life, there is a wonderful power hidden in man's soul – if only it was discovered! What makes man helpless is the ignorance of the power of freewill in him. This is the mighty power, the God power, hidden in man. Therefore it is a most wonderful power.

It is the ignorance of this that keeps man in darkness with regard to his divine heritage, and every difficulty he meets with through life – owing to life's limitations – covers that divine spark of freewill in him. In time it becomes obscure to his view, and this culminates in the tragedy of life.

Can a soul after death see conditions which were hidden from it during its earthly life?

Certainly. Death is the unveiling of a cover, after which there are many things that will be known to the soul, which have been so far hidden from it in regard to its own life and in regard to the whole world.

Can these *djinn*-souls also attain mastership or reach spiritual attainment?

Yes, they all do, some more than others. But, as I have said before – and I shall repeat it a thousand times – not only the souls of angels, *djinns* and human beings, but even animals and birds, trees and plants, and the smallest germ and insect – all have a spiritual fulfilment in their life, and if that were not so, life would be a waste. No creature that has ever been born on earth, however bad or wrong it may seem to be, will be deprived of that spiritual bliss. It is only a matter of time: there is a difference in the process through which one has to touch the bliss. As I have said: as human beings with their different planes of evolution – however bad or miserable they are – will have a moment, a day, when they touch that spiritual bliss, so even the animals – carnivorous or herbivorous, birds or insects – all have a moment of promise, and that promise is the fulfilment of the purpose of their lives. Even if an insect has been born to live for one moment, yet the purpose of that moment has been accomplished.

By this we understand that there is nothing in this world which is here without a purpose. By this we learn that, although our place in the scheme of life and our work in this plan of the whole universe may seem different one from the other, yet in the sum total of things we all – as the lower creation, together with the *djinns* and the angels – have one and the same result: that result is the realization of truth in greater or smaller degree, and this realization comes to all in the form of bliss.

CHAPTER 9

21st August, 1923, 5.30 p.m.

THE *djinn* world is a universe of minds; it may be called a mental world. Yet the soul is with the mind; the soul with the mind is called spirit, and therefore it may also be called a spiritual world.

The questions: what are the *djinns* like, what do they look like? – may be answered in the same way as in explaining the form of angels: that things are not always as they are, but also as we see them. Man always pictures the beings he imagines and cannot see with his physical eyes as something like himself; or man's imagination may gather together different forms, for instance wings from the birds, horns from the oxen, hooves from horses and paws from tigers. He puts them all together and makes a new form. It is beyond possibility to explain exactly what the *djinns* look like, and yet there is no being in existence which lives without a form. In support of man's imagination which pictures the angel or the *djinn* more or less in the form of man, there is much that can be said. For everything in the world proves at the end of examination that it is striving to culminate in the form of man. The rocks and the trees, fruits and flowers, mountains and clouds, all show a gradual development towards the image of man. A keen observer of nature will prove this a thousand times. There is everything in the world to support this argument. Every form shows either a part of the human form or an undeveloped outline of it. As it is with material things, so it is with the lower creation, and in the same way it is towards the human form that even the form of the *djinn* and the angel is growing. It is this idea which is spoken of in the Scriptures in the words: 'We have made man in Our Own image.' If I were to add a word of explanation, I would say: 'We have made all forms in order to complete the image of man'.

The world of the *djinns* is the world of mind. Yet the minds of the *djinns* are not so developed as the minds of men. The reason is that the experience of life on the earth completes the making of the mind. In the *djinn* world the mind is only a design, an outline, a design which is not yet embroidered.

What is the occupation of the *djinns*? What does the world of the *djinns* look like? One may give a thousand explanations, but nothing can explain it fully. For instance, if a person were to ask me what China looks like, I would say: 'Most wonderful, most interesting'. But if he said: 'What is wonderful and interesting there?', I would say: 'Go and take a tour through China in order that you may see it fully'. We have not sufficient words to explain what the *djinn* is like, or what the world of the *djinn* is. What little can be said about it, is that it is a world of music, a world of art, a world of poetry, a world of intelligence, cheerfulness and joy, a world of thought, imagination and sentiment, a world that a poet would long for and a musician would crave to experience. The life of the *djinn* is the ideal life for a thinker, a life which is free from all illness, pure from all bitterness of human nature, free to move about in through space without any hindrance; a most joyful place, where the Sun of Intelligence shines, where the trouble of birth and death is not so severe, life not so short as on the earth. If there is any paradise, it is the world of the *djinns*. Hindus have called it *Indra-loka* and pictured *Gandharvas* and _ *Apsaras*[26] there; a paradise of which every prophet has spoken to his followers in the way they could understand.

The question: how does a prophet know of this? – may be answered by saying that the soul of the prophet is like a fruit which, by its weight, touches the ground. It has not dropped on to the earth like other fruits, it is still connected with the branch to which it is attached, the branch which droops through all the planes of existence. So he, in his experience of the different planes, so to speak, touches all the different worlds. It is this mystery which is hidden behind the prophetic genius and the prophetic inspiration. It is through this current that the fruit is connected with the stem.[27] Therefore, though on the earth, the prophet speaks of heaven, though on the earth, he calls aloud the name of God. While to many God is an imagination, to him God is the reality.

> Do the *djinns* communicate with the spirits returning from the earth?
>
> Yes, they do communicate. At the same time the inhabitants of a certain country, who are pure from the knowledge of other countries, are much happier in their own surroundings and in their own way, and if some go out and bring knowledge of other countries, they do not like it. It destroys their knowledge and their peace: it is not agreeable to them. It is in the same way with the *djinns*.

CHAPTER 10

22nd August, 1923, 3.30 p.m.

[28]THE day when science discovers the secret of electricity fully, on that day science will also discover the secret of the soul, for the secret of the soul is not very far from the secret of electricity. For instance, what the current of electricity attracts to it and which gives light, is not necessarily electricity. Electricity is that power which is hidden there in the current, not that which is manifest.

If that is understood, then the explanation of the soul will be the same. The body is composed of atoms attracted from the world in which the body exists: in the physical world physical atoms, attracted by some secret current. That secret current is the soul. Upon it is one globe over another. There is something within the body, but at the same time all is collected and gathered upon the current which is within, and that current is the soul, the ray of the divine Sun. One can also understand that this current in the heavenly spheres, in the angelic sphere, attracts angelic atoms, heavenly atoms, in the *djinn* sphere *djinn* atoms, and in the physical sphere physical atoms.

Therefore mankind is already dressed in the angelic dress over which he has put the dress of the *djinn*, and over the dress of the *djinn* he has put the dress of the human being. He really has all three dresses, one over the other. When he sees the dress of the human being, he thinks he is a human being. Now that he no longer sees the dresses of the two other worlds, he imagines that he has not got them. But they are there!

CHAPTER 11

22nd August, 1923, 5.30 p.m.

THE soul is a current. We may call it an electric current, yet it is unlike the electric current we know on this physical plane, different from it in its power and phenomena, a current which runs more speedily than anything we know, a current which is beyond time and space, a current which runs through all the planes of life.

If manifestation is the Breath of God, the souls are breaths of God. According to the conception of the Yogi, there is one breath and there are many breaths. The one breath, which is the central breath, is called by Yogis *prāna*, and all other breaths, which have a certain part to play in the mechanism of the human body, are lesser breaths. Again *prāna* and all other breaths put together make one breath, which we call life. The souls therefore are different breaths of God and all different breaths put together make one breath, a divine Breath, which is Life. This idea may be pictured as a tree which has a stem and various branches, each branch in its place representing a stem.[29]

The elements of every sphere are different. Just as the air of every part of the world is different, the water is different, the earth is different, their effect upon the human being is different, so the atoms of every plane are different. Their nature and character are as different as their effect. Therefore the form of the angel need not be compared in any way with the form of the *djinn*; neither can the form of the *djinn* be compared with the form of man, for the atoms of which the *djinn* is made belong to another sphere.

A man who is accustomed to physical forms cannot very well grasp the idea of the forms of the *djinns*. This shows us that the soul shoots forth and functions in a body which each particular sphere offers it. The heavens, for instance, offer that luminous body to the soul which in Sufi terms is called *nūr*, because heaven is made of luminous atoms: it is all illumination. It was the recognition of that angelic body in the Buddha which caused his disciples to make the statue of

Buddha in gold. Often artists have had the conception of painting angels in gold, for gold represents light.

The soul that goes as far as the sphere of the *djinn*, as a current coming from the heavens, functions in a body of the *djinn* world. The question is: a soul which comes from the heavens, from the world of angels, does it come to the *djinn* world without a body? The answer is: No, it comes with a body, the angelic body. Yet it becomes necessary for the souls, coming with the angelic body into the *djinn* world, to don a body of that particular world in order to stand the weather of that plane. Animals which live in cold countries have a different skin from those which live in a tropical climate. That is the condition for going into any other sphere. Even if a person were journeying, going from a tropical country to another tropical country, and on the way had to pass through a cold climate, he would need suitable garments for that climate. What is the body? The body is a garment of the soul. The soul wears this garment in order to stand the weather of that particular sphere.

Souls which are passing through the *djinn* sphere towards the physical planes and which do not stop in that sphere, meet with other travellers who are on their journey back home, and they learn from them a great many things. There is give and take, there is buying and selling, there is learning and teaching. But who teaches the most? The one with more experience, the one who is going back home. This latter gives the map of the journey to the soul travelling towards manifestation. It is from this map that the travelling soul strikes its path, rightly or wrongly. One soul may have one instruction, another soul may have more instructions, one soul may be clear, another may be puzzled; yet they all go forward as the travellers of a caravan, taking with them all the precious information, all the things they have learned from the others on the journey.

It is for this reason that every child born on earth possesses, besides what he has inherited from his parents and ancestors, a power and knowledge quite peculiar to himself and different from that which his parents and ancestors possessed. Yet he knows not when and whence he received it, or who gave him that knowledge. But he shows from the beginning of his life on earth signs of having known things which he has never been taught.

THE SOUL WHENCE AND WHITHER

One soul is more impressionable than another. One soul is perhaps more impressed by the angelic heavens, and that impression has remained deeper in that soul throughout the whole journey. Another is more impressed by the sphere of the *djinns*, and that impression lasts with the soul all through the journey. Then there is another soul which is not deeply impressed with the angelic heavens or the *djinn* world. That soul does not know of these worlds, it comes through blindly and is only interested in things of the earth when it reaches it. One generally finds among artists, poets, musicians, thinkers, writers, philosophers, as well as among inventors, administrators, and great politicians, souls of the *djinn* world who have brought with them on to the earth some deep impression which causes them in their lives to be geniuses.

Impression is a great phenomenon in itself. 'As a man thinketh, so he is.' And what does man think? He thinks that with which he is most impressed. And what he is most impressed with, that he himself is. Do we not see in our life on earth that people who are deeply impressed with a certain personality, ideal, thought or feeling, become in time the same? If this is true, what is man? Man *is* his impression. The soul impressed deeply in the *djinn* world by some personality coming back from the earth – an impression deeply engraved upon that soul, which it can never throw away – certainly becomes that personality with which it is impressed. Suppose a soul was impressed in the *djinn* world with the personality of Beethoven. When born on earth, he is Beethoven in thought, in feeling, in tendency, in inclination, in knowledge. Only in addition to that personality he has the heritage of his parents and of his ancestors. As the son of a certain family is called by the name of the same family, so the impression of a certain personality may rightfully be called by the name of the same personality. Therefore, if Shankarāchārya[30] claimed to be the reincarnation* of Shiva, there is every reason for his claim, as this theory stands in support of it.

Life from the beginning to the end is a mystery. The deeper one dives in order to investigate the truth, the greater difficulty one finds in distinguishing what is called individuality. But it is not the aim of the wise to hold on to individuality: wisdom lies in understanding the secret of individuality, its

---

* See Appendix on Reincarnation – p.191

composition or its decomposition, which resolves in the end into one individuality, the Individuality of God.

'There is one God, none exists save He.'

> You spoke of *prāna* as the central breath. Would you explain what that means?

> There is a river and there are many streams that branch out of the river; they are small rivers. So is breath: there is one central breath and many other breaths. The one breath keeps the mechanism of the whole body going but there are many other breaths: for instance, those which help in contraction and expansion, also in sneezing, yawning or blinking the eyes. All this comes from a certain direction of a little breath, a stream branching out from the central breath which works as a battery behind all the mechanical actions and movements of the body.

> Are there still other worlds besides the angelic and the *djinn* world which impress the soul going towards manifestation?

> No, these two worlds specially.

> Do the souls on their way to manifestation know that they are to experience life on the physical plane, and do they look forward to that experience?

> They do not know distinctly, they know and they do not know. There is an unceasing impulse to go forward, to experience what they may be able to experience, to know what they may be able to know, and to reach the place they may be able to reach. It is that tendency which gives the soul the power to advance. Those which are able to go forward to reach the physical sphere manifest as human beings.

> If the *djinn* plane is so beautiful and pure, how is it that any *djinn* coming to the earth can be impressed with evil? Where does it learn evil?

> The path of the *djinn* is the path of beauty. But this is not only the path of the *djinn*: the path of every soul is the path of beauty, and every good soul and bad

soul is seeking after beauty. When it steps wrongly in the pursuit of beauty, we call it evil and when it steps rightly in the pursuit of beauty, we call it virtue.

As is said in the Qur'an: 'God is beautiful and He loves beauty'.

The souls which manifest on earth, must they attain perfection on the earth, or can they also attain it on the journey towards the goal?

Yes, it can be attained on the journey to the goal also, but I should think that what is done today is better than to-morrow. Imagine a man who is going to a foreign country and remembers in the train that he must learn the language! If we can realize perfection to-day, it is better than waiting to attain it in the hereafter.

Can a soul choose its place of birth and its family?

Yes, it chooses nearly always.

If one soul meets Beethoven in the *djinn* world, and another meets Beethoven in the angelic world, is the impression different?

Certainly it is different; for after manifestation on earth one will show the soul of Beethoven, the other his mind.

So there may be many incarnations of Beethoven?

Yes.

CHAPTER 12

24th August, 1923, 5.30 p.m.

SOULS which are impressed in the *djinn* world by the personalities of those they meet on their way towards manifestation receive different kinds of impressions. Some are deeply impressed by one personality and some are slightly impressed. Some souls receive many impressions on that plane and it is hardly distinguishable which impression has more effect and which less. However, it is certainly true that in reality one impression is predominant in every soul. The soul, so to speak, conceives this impression, an impression which is not only the outline of the personality which impresses it, but is the very essence of that personality which this soul has absorbed. A soul may not be compared with an object, for the soul is all the life there is. Therefore it not only takes an impression like a photographic plate but it becomes nurtured with it. The soul is creative, therefore it expresses all that it has absorbed on its way.

The question: is a *djinn* sent to earth on a mission to human beings – may be answered: yes, whether angel, or *djinn*, or man, all are intended to play their part in the working scheme of the whole universe, and all are used by the wisdom of God for the purpose for which they were created. No doubt the angels are primarily for the angelic heavens and the *djinns* for the sphere of the *djinns*; yet, in a house the inhabitants of the second or third floor are sometimes sent to the ground floor on an errand, when it is necessary. The most remarkable thing that one notices in all those planes of existence, is that the beings of these distinct planes are not imprisoned there by the Creator. They become captive themselves, just as a man who lives in a village passes his whole life in the same place and when told of the history of the neighbouring country, it is for him as another world: he never tries to leave his village, and the neighbouring country is foreign to him. He has heard the name of the country all through his life, but he has never made it possible for him to visit it. It is this nature of the soul which arises from its ignorance that limits the soul which is, in point of fact, limitless.

How does the soul of a *djinn* communicate with human beings on earth? It focuses itself upon the heart of man and experiences all that the man experiences and knows all that the man knows. It is easy for a *djinn* to do this, because its mind is as clear as crystal, and it can accommodate and reflect all that falls within its range of vision.

One might ask: if the souls on their return journey from the earth give their experience to the souls coming from above, what do the souls coming from above give to the souls on their return journey? They can do a great deal too, for they know the forgotten ways through which they have recently travelled, and the laws and customs of the way that the souls on the return journey need to learn. Besides this, they give to them that light and life which is necessary to those worn-out and withered souls which have probably given most of themselves to this ever robbing and consuming plane of the earth. In this way a man is helped onwards towards his goal by the soul he meets on the way in his own return journey.

The question: in what manner can *djinns* help man on the earth? – may be answered by saying that they are capable of inspiring man, not with a definite knowledge of things, but with the sense of the knowledge, especially of the knowledge of art and beauty, of tone and rhythm, the knowledge of inventive nature, and sometimes with a sense of knowledge that might help to accomplish great things in life. But though they meet as inhabitants of different countries who do not know the language, it is still the language of the heart which becomes the medium of communication.

Heart talks to heart, and soul speaks to soul.

> How can the soul, which is the divine ray, get worn-out and withered?

> It is not the soul which gets worn-out and withered: it is what it has gathered around it and what it has imagined itself to be. All that it has taken from the lower plane is subjected to the laws of the lower plane. So it is not the real self which is worn-out and withered, but the false self.

> Can we say 'higher' or 'lower' speaking of planes?

> We may say 'higher' for our convenience, but we cannot say 'higher' in the sense of 'preferable'. We do not know what is preferable. I should say that the human plane is preferable to all, because there is the sum total of the whole creation: it is the fulfilment of the whole creation. Therefore, the person who shows a ripened human personality – that is the thing which is desirable.

> Can a soul ask for help and advice of a soul which it meets on its journey towards manifestation?

> No, it cannot ask for advice and help, because its

mind is not like a human mind. But it is passive, and so it gets it without asking. Being passive, one soul will respond more than another soul. The child in its infancy never asks for anything. It learns to ask later. It takes whatever it sees and feels it at first, it only wants to have it. That is the nature of the soul.

Can a *djinn* attract a soul on earth in order to experience earthly life? Can a soul on earth, who has a great desire to accomplish something, attract a *djinn* to help it?

Yes, both things are possible. A soul may attract a *djinn* to help it on earth, and a *djinn* may attract a soul to accomplish something the *djinn* wants to accomplish.

Why is the *djinn* sufficiently interested in the thing it is going to accomplish on the earth?

There is no special interest for a *djinn* to accomplish anything on earth; but when it sees what is going on on earth, then it becomes interested. A person who does not go out of the house, has no interest out of the house; but, if the window is opened, he gets interested.

What is the difference between the real *djinn* and the *djinn*-like human being? Is there any visible mark of the *djinn* in the *djinn*-like human being?

There is no resemblance between the two. The *djinn* which is in the *djinn* plane is quite different as a *djinn*, and the *djinn*-like human being is no more a *djinn* but a human being. However, a soul which is most impressed by the *djinn* plane – that soul has much of the *djinn* plane when it comes on earth. Even in face and features that soul will show something of the *djinn* on earth. Also, a soul coming from the angelic plane who was most impressed by that plane, when born on earth will show this in his face, his nature and character.

There is something common in the human face and features and when there is some little look out of the common, then this is the sign of another world.

Also in the nature and character – if that nature and character are common, it is just like every human being; if there is something uncommon, then that is the sign of the *djinn* plane or of the angelic plane. There is something very beautiful in uncommon things, something to admire and to observe.

Does not the idea that the worlds of the angels and *djinns* are enriched by the experience rising up from the life on earth suggest that the Being of God may also be affected and recreated in this way?

The Being of God is a perfect Being. The experience and riches that the souls bring from the earth by knowledge or by anything is no addition to God. For God it is only that something which is in the hand has come up to the elbow. What difference does it make? It is the same! On the other side it is better that the things of the hand be in the hand, not in the elbow. As it is said in the Qur'an: 'All the treasures of earth and heaven belong to God'. It exists already, is already in Him, the perfect Being.

What then is the reason why God moves souls from one plane to another?

Because it is His nature. By this He experiences His satisfaction from the fulfilment of the purpose of the whole creation. But satisfaction is not knowledge. It is something which belongs to Him but is brought to fulfilment. In the same way, joy is not something brought from outside; it belongs to the soul, but it is aroused by a certain movement, a certain action. It is not brought about by that action, it is in us, it belongs to us. The action brings us the realization. So it is with the whole creation: the creation is an action which brings to God that satisfaction for which it was created.

When God is not creative, does that mean that He is unconscious? Why does God want to be conscious?

This creation does not bring something new to God: it makes Him only conscious of what He is. The consciousness must have something to become conscious of, otherwise it is consciousness in essence only. A man who is in a dark room with his eyes open sees nothing. That does not mean that his eyes are incapable of seeing, but that there is nothing to be seen. The eyes possess the power of sight, but they become conscious of sight by having something to see. So creation makes God conscious of what He is, conscious of Himself.

It is most interesting to watch how that nature of God works in man. For instance, sometimes a person begins to walk about the room, or to play the drum on the table, or to look up and down, or to rub his hands, when there is no need for it. Why does he do it? Because the absence of action has the effect of paralysing the activity of the mind; when the absence of activity has paralysed the mind, then the soul begins to feel lonely and begins to wonder whether it is living or not living. When the person begins to tap or to walk, then it realizes: no, no, I am living, because it lives in the outward sensation and its outward sensation gives it consciousness of life. If we think about this more, it opens up a vast field of knowledge, the deepest knowledge possible: God's desire to feel Himself.

But do these actions not show restlessness?

Restlessness in the case of man, but if it is God, it is activity.

There are two things: there is weakness and there is strength. When a person is weak he is always keeping up some activity and acts without any control. But on the other side, strength and inspiration also make one do something, accomplish something. These two things are quite different.

When God is not conscious, is He nothing?

Why nothing? How can anything come out of nothing? When we are not doing some active work, we are still doing a greater work. In sleep we are sometimes conscious in our being. When God is unconscious, He is conscious in His own Being.

CHAPTER 13

7th September, 1923, 5.30 p.m.

HAS the sphere of the *djinn* many worlds, in the same way as there are planets in our universe? Yes, many, and different from one another, as the planets in our universe are different; yet not so far apart, not so much out of communication with each other as in our universe.

Is the heaven of the angels created on the same model? Yes, but is it not on the model of the heaven of the angels that our universe has been moulded, and also that of the *djinns*?

What is the life there? What is it like? It is difficult to explain, and difficult to put into words but, for example, one might see the difference in the life of the birds which can fly over seas and forests, over hills and dales, and feel in tune with nature and express their joy in song. Then the deer in the woods, dwelling in the caves of the mountains, drinking water at the natural springs, moving about in the open spaces, looking at the horizon from morning till evening, the sun their time-keeper and the moon serving as their torch. Imagine then our lives, the lives of human beings in crowded cities, days in the factories and nights indoors; away from God, away from nature, even away from Self; a life fully absorbed in the struggle for existence, an ever increasing struggle to which there is no end. There is the picture before us, for us to imagine what life the angels live in the highest heaven, what life the *djinns* live in the middle heaven, and for us to compare with their lives our life as human beings in our universe.

Are there suns? Are there moons in their worlds, as we have in ours? Yes, this outer solar system is the reflection of the inner solar system.

What difference is there between time, the conception of time, such as we have and the idea of time they have there? There is an incomparable difference. No words will give the exact idea of the comparison between these conceptions of time but, for the sake of convenience, let us say that our year is the hour of the *djinns* and a moment of the angels.

Are there angels and *djinns* of longer and shorter lives, as

64

with men on earth? Certainly there are, but there is no comparison between the time of their life and that of human beings.

Are there differences among the *djinns* and among the angels, as among men of different kinds? Indeed there are, but among the *djinns* not so many as among men; still less among the angels.

What about the time that every soul spends in the heavens of the angels and in the sphere of the *djinns*? The speed of every soul is different. It is according to the speed with which they manifest; it is a different dimension. The difference of speed is like travelling on the earth, sailing on the water, and flying through the air. Difference of speed between different souls may be likened to one child advancing in its thought so that it may learn in ten years things which another could not learn in a hundred years of life on earth. Nevertheless, as they say: 'slow and sure'. Souls with balance and rhythm throughout their manifestation learn and experience much more than by a rapid run through the heavens.

> Is it one's choice to be rapid rather than slow, or is it a question of temperament?
>
> I should say it is a question of temperament, but I think that the happy medium is the best. Too slow is monotonous and too quick is undesirable. I think the joy of the journey is in the balance of it. If man travelled with the speed of an ant, or a worm, or a germ – no doubt eternity is before him, but it would not be interesting for a man. He is not made to travel in that way. Therefore the man who adopts an artificial speed is always limited. A person who goes in an aeroplane or in a train will not enjoy the full pleasure of the journey, as the man does who travels on foot. The man who travels in the train cannot imagine to what extent the one who walks can enjoy it, because that is his natural speed.
>
> Besides, in everything we can see the same thing. From the grammophone we hear the human voice, but it loses its magnetism because it is the human voice which is made to strike directly upon the ears, it is the human voice which gives the full joy to the

human being. When it comes from the grammophone, – that spoils it.

Do the *djinn* and angelic worlds occupy the same space as our world and do they pervade it?

The question of space is difficult to answer in words. The reason is that we think of all other aspects of space in the same way as we think of the space we are accustomed to know as such.

For instance, there is little said about the space which is in the iris, in the pupil of the eye, so small and yet so vastly accommodating. If the space is so accommodating in that little pupil of the eye – so little if we can measure it according to our idea of space – what is the explanation of space as an accommodation? If this tiny place, the pupil, is so accommodating that thousands of miles can come in it and it can accommodate them all, then there is another aspect of space, different than what we are accustomed to know as such. When this idea becomes clear to man, then the vision of the heavens is opened before him. A Chinese philosopher, when answering the question: 'what is the soul like?' said: 'like the iris, the pupil of the eye'. This means that it is accommodation, it is space itself.

And think of the heart. If there were a thousand universes, it would accommodate them all, it is so large. Although every person knows the word 'heart', he cannot realize what 'heart' is. If he knew it, he would say with Asif[31] the mystic: 'What is the earth, and the whole cosmos? If the doors of the heart were open, the heart would prove to be larger than the whole universe'.

What little one can say is by showing the picture of the cross. There is a horizontal space and there is the other kind of space, which can be pictured as a perpendicular line. This is not the same space, it is quite a different space, and it is to explain this space that the mystics and seers have used the word 'within'; to explain the horizontal space they have used the word 'without'.

THE SOUL TOWARDS MANIFESTATION

What is the fourth dimension?

I use the word dimension in the sense of a different space, a space the character of which is different. If I say different dimension, this is the accommodation which is in the space; for instance, in the iris is a different accommodation or space.

If we call this earthly sphere one dimension, the sphere of the *djinn* a second and the sphere of the angel a third, the sphere of God is the fourth. So if we do not use the word dimension in the sense of length, breadth and height, then the fourth is that which is sought after.

Are there not three different kinds of space and three different kinds of time?

If you say that there are four dimensions, I will say that there are four. If you say that there are three kinds of space, then I will say that there are three: this sphere, the sphere of the *djinns* and the sphere of the angels.

Then there is another aspect according to the explanation of four dimensions: the length, the breadth and the height, and besides that the fourth dimension, which the mystic calls 'within'.

There came a scientist one day to hear my lecture. He was interested in some of my ideas, but he asked: 'If you say "in the body", I can understand it, but when you say "within", I cannot understand what you mean'. I explained: what is space? Space is that which accommodates; that is the definition of space. Your mind is a space also, it accommodates, it is a space that is wider than the world. Your eye is a space also. But the mind is not necessarily the brain, nor are the eyes, which outwardly appear, the only space. Behind them is another space connected with the eyes. Therefore the eye is a road between man and God; therefore it is 'I', it means: 'self'. It has a different spelling, but it is the same thing. It is the ego, it sees. What sees? God Himself sees through it. Therefore there is a direct road between the earth and the heaven through the eyes.

The eyes which appear before us are two, the sight is one: that is the third eye. The third eye is where the two eyes are linked together and become one. This is the key to the Egyptian mystery where there is the sign of the eye. In that eye there is the eye and the 'I', the ego, both.

When we say that there are three different kinds of space, naturally there are three kinds of time that are incomparable. The times of the higher heavens are more durable, are longer, compared with the times of this world. The time of the highest heaven is still longer. Therefore, there are three different worlds and three different times. However, to the one who realizes the ultimate truth, time and space – both – are of little importance, he rises above it. This yard and foot and inch is nothing, once you begin to look at the horizon; and once you begin to think of eternity, day, month or year is nothing.

Is time an aspect of space?

It is. By space time becomes intelligible and by time space becomes intelligible. But when one has insight into life, neither time nor space stands before him, for both of these have created this illusion which we call life.

Furthermore, rhythm cannot exist without tone, nor can tone exist without rhythm. They are interdependent for their existence. So are time and space.

To what extent is the difference of the speed of the souls?

The difference of the journey in every heaven is incomparable. The speed is much quicker in the higher world, compared with the lower world. It is quickest in the heavens of the angels.

And when you compare two souls in the same sphere?

There can be a very great difference, an immense difference between two souls in the same sphere. The difference among the angels may be ten thousands of years in their attainment.

PART II

Manifestation or
The Manifested Soul

The Arrival of the Soul on the Physical Plane

THE ARRIVAL OF THE SOUL ON THE PHYSICAL PLANE

CHAPTER 14

25th August, 1923, 5.30 p.m.

AFTER the soul has passed through the sphere of the *djinns* it arrives on the physical plane. What helps the soul to come on to the physical plane? What opens the way for this new coming soul to enter physical existence? It is the souls on earth. The coming soul enters the physical sphere by the channel of the breath – the breath which is the power at the back of every action. It works as a battery which keeps the physical mechanism of the human body going. The secret of birth and death is to be found in the mystery of breath.

What is Cupid[23]? It is the soul which is being born. Before it appears on the physical plane it is pictured by the wise as Cupid, an angel. It is an angel, for the soul itself is the angel. Duality in every aspect of life and on whatever plane is creative, and its issue is the purpose, the outcome, of the dual aspect of nature. The affinity which brings about the fulfilment of the purpose is the phenomenon of Cupid. In reality it is the phenomenon of the soul.

When the soul is born on earth its first expression is a cry. Why does it cry? Because it finds itself in a new place which is all strange to it. It finds itself in captivity, which it did not experience before. Every person, every object is something new, something foreign to this soul, but soon this condition passes away. No sooner do the senses of the infant become acquainted with the outer life, which so continually attracts its attention, than it first becomes interested in breathing the air of the world, then in hearing the sounds, then in seeing the objects before it, then in touching them, and then its taste develops. The more familiar the soul becomes with this physical world, the more interested it becomes, though sometimes it shows homesickness in the fits of crying that it so often has during its infancy. It is not always illness, it is not

71

always that it is crying for things outside itself. No doubt, as it grows it longs for things outside itself, but it often cries from the feeling of having been removed from a place which was more pleasant and comfortable, and having come to a foreign land of which it knows so little. It is this which causes the infant to have fits of crying.

The wisdom of nature is perfect, and there is no better vision of the splendour of the divine wisdom for the thinker than an infant in its early infancy. If the senses of an infant were developed as are the senses of a grown-up person, it would lose its reason from the sudden pressure of the physical world falling instantly upon it. Its delicate senses would not be able to withstand the pressure of the many various and intense activities of this world. How marvellously does the wisdom behind it work – evidence of that divine Protector, Father-and-Mother, the Creator, Who is the support and protection of all – so that the senses of the child develop gradually. As the infant becomes more familiar with life, the more its senses are developed. The more it knows, the more its mind expands, and it cannot know more than its mind can grasp. So in every way an infant is protected in both mind and body.

Is the affinity which brings two human beings together in love always the soul working behind?

Certainly.

Are man and woman always separated, or are they two halves of one entity which have been separated and have to be reunited before arriving at the goal?

You may call them two parts of one soul, but really speaking we are all parts of one soul and we all long to unite in one soul, to meet in the One Soul which is the ideal and goal.

At the same time there are affinities; affinities of the *djinn* plane, of the angelic plane, of the human plane; many different ties, many different affinities of souls which attract them to one another.

Will you tell us something about twins? Why are they not always united on earth?

They are meant to be united. If twins are twins in

the real sense of the word – that is, if two friend-souls have started the whole journey together and have managed to come together on earth – they are most united. I have known twins so united, that if one had an illness, the other had the same illness; if one was happy, the other was happy also, even if they were separated in space. But then there could be two persons walking in the rain and, finding some shelter, they happened to arrive in the same place. That is another thing.

Again there may be two souls born in different countries, brought up by different parents, belonging to different races and nations, and yet their thought and mind and feeling may be akin. They would attract one another, they would supply to one another what is needed in their lives. They may be man and woman, or man and man, or woman and woman, they can be best friends, they can be good partners, they may even be in the capacity of master and servant, but they are twin-souls, true twin-souls.

Why are some souls, coming to the physical plane, born in such miserable surroundings?

There is a saying in the Qur-an: 'The Creation has come out of darkness.' The soul does not always come with open eyes; it comes with closed eyes, the picture of which the infant shows whose eyes open afterwards. To compare one condition with another condition one need to be familiar with the conditions, and that time comes after being born.

If this question is considered more deeply, one will come to a very great realization of the secret of life, especially of good fortune and bad fortune. Then one will know that there is not always a design in which the soul is so limited that it cannot get out of it, but that every soul makes for itself a condition, even after coming on earth. Are there not thousands and thousands who live in miserable, in bad conditions because they know no better? If they had known better, they would have managed to become

73

better. This rule applies to all kinds of people. They say: 'There are so many miseries in my life', but most of the reasons for misery are in their own helplessness and ignorance. If they knew how to combat, how to get out of misery – there are many possibilities that may open the doors, many ways to get out of it, and it is never too late.

To me just now it does not seem unfair when I see bad conditions around a person, because I see that his gains have equal losses and his losses equal gains: it sums up. Only we do not see how much are the costs and whether the costs come first, or last, or in the middle. Outward conditions count little.

CHAPTER 15

27th August, 1923, 5.30 p.m.

WHEN the soul comes into the physical world it receives an offering from the whole universe, and that offering is the body in which to function. It is not offered to the soul only by the parents, but by the ancestors, by the nation and race into which the soul is born, and by the whole human race. This body is not only an offering by the human race, but is an outcome of something that the whole world has produced for ages: a clay which has been kneaded a thousand times over; a clay which has been prepared so that in its every development it has become more intelligent, more radiant and more living; a clay which appeared first in the mineral kingdom, which developed in the vegetable kingdom, which then appeared as the animal kingdom, and which was finished in the making of that body which is offered to the new coming human soul.

One may ask: 'Is it not true then, as some scientists say in their biological study, that man has risen from the animal kingdom?' Certainly it is true, but true in the sense explained above. In order to come to the world of human beings a soul need not be an animal and then develop itself in man. We need not understand by this that every rock turned into a plant, every plant became an animal, and every animal turned into a man. The soul is direct from heaven, it functions in a body and it is this body through which it experiences life on the earth more fully. Rocks and trees and animals, therefore, may not be considered as the ancestors of the soul. It is the body which is the outcome of the working of all these different kingdoms, which are the development of one another.

A question arises: 'Why must a soul function in a human body, why not in an animal, in a bird, in an insect?' The answer is that it does so function. Every soul is not the same ray, has not the same degree of illumination, the same far reaching power, the same volume of Light. Therefore it is true that souls do not only function in a human body, but in all forms, however insignificant and small, which seem living.

Then there is the question: 'What about rocks and mountains, and what about the sea and the river? Where have they come from? Are they not all the outcome of the soul?' The answer is that nature in general in its various aspects is the materialization of that Light which is called Spirit, the divine Spirit. 'But has it a soul? Has everything in nature a soul?' The answer is: not in the sense of the word soul as we understand it, for we recognize only that ray which functions in the human body as a soul; we do not recognize the ray which functions in the lower creation to be the same, although it is a ray which has come from the same source.

There are two things: there are rays and there is Light from which they spring. If the rays are the souls of living beings, then the Light of that same divine Sun is the Spirit of the whole of nature. It is the same Light, it is the same Spirit, but not divided and not distinct as are the rays which we call souls.

Now the question arises: 'Why has nature its different aspects? There is earth and there is water, and there are mountains, and there is the sea. If the Spirit behind it is one, why is it all distinct and different?' The answer is that creation is a gradual evolution of that Light which is the source and goal of all things. For instance, plant life is a development of the mineral kingdom of the earth; animal life is the development of the vegetable kingdom; human life is the culmination of this evolution. But this culmination is the finishing of that vehicle which the soul uses. By this evolution the soul is not evolved, by this evolution is only meant that the soul has adopted a more finished instrument in order to experience life more fully. No doubt, the better the instrument, the greater the satisfaction of the soul. When one looks from this point of view at the whole creation, one feels like saying that not only man, but the whole manifestation was created in the image of God.

Why does part of the Light become rays of human souls, and does the other part remain in plants and animals?

No, I did not mean that the other part remains plants and animals. I have only said that where there is no individual or separate appearance, but where there is a mass of matter before us – as the earth, a lake, or a river, or a mountain, or the sea – there we see the Light of the same divine Sun acting in its radiant form. There is Intelligence also. But the ray is a kind of straight, living current, and it is this living current, functioning in a more developed body, which is able to produce that experience which is the fulfilment of the whole creation. As soon as the trees begin to appear as separate entities, no doubt there are separate rays.

It is most difficult to differentiate the rays from Light and Light from the rays. It is more for the convenience of our understanding. It is all Light; in the rays it is more separate, more distinct; in the Light it is more collective, more together. Therefore, all that is before our eyes as something connected together, is the phenomenon of that Light, and all that shows itself as an entity, is expressive of the ray.

One must remember that the truth cannot be put into words. What one can do, is to make as much as possible an effort to make the mystery of life intelligible to the mind. Therefore the words Light and ray and Sun are useful, but it must be understood by the light of one's intuition, and then I do not doubt that this problem will become clear to one's sight.

Why do some rays become trees, some human beings?

Some rays, falling, functioned upon the perfect body and became human beings, some rays functioned upon the other bodies and became trees and plants and minerals. Take, for instance, the example of the rain. Why must the raindrops rear the poisonous plants and the weeds? Why should they not fall only upon the corn, fruits and flowers? The rain falls on all things, on the more useful and the less useful plants. So do the rays coming from above. Some fall on the street, some on rocks, some on the fertile soil – and there they grow. Therefore if we picture them as a divine rain, this will show us that this divine rain, falling in the form of Light, falls everywhere without distinction, takes up everything that is there, and raises all that comes out of it.

Can you explain when and how the difference in the development of the soul comes in the different kingdoms?

The body is not dead matter. It is matter with spirit. That spirit is Light. One cannot make a very great distinction between the differences and the grades of Light. If the degree of Light of a soul was not developed to a certain point in the body that the soul would meet on its way to its expression, the soul would not take it; it would be attracted to another body developed up to another point. There are numerous differences between the rays. Rays are first expressed, and then they fall upon all that meets them. The differences of the rays are that they are not of the same grade of intensity, of illumination, of expression.

Souls are first expressed. There is nothing to attract them. Then influences come, and the souls go where they are attracted: to the mineral, the vegetable, the animal or the human kingdom. The ray that falls in the human kingdom is more intense and direct.

Is the attraction of the body towards the ray or soul

entirely by accident? Is there not an element of justice?★

The idea of justice is based upon good and bad. Where there is justice, there is injustice. That means: there are two. Truth is only one. The idea of justice and injustice is from man's conception. When a person rises above justice and injustice, which is subject to change in his every evolution – when he gets above this – he will reach the knowledge of truth. Our conception of fairness and unfairness belongs to our particular evolution. The less intelligent a man is, the more he sees fairness and unfairness, and the more he thinks about it. A stupid person is always ready to judge. In heaven there is only truth and truth is one; where there is no comparison, there is no fairness and no unfairness. Something is greater than fairness and unfairness, and that is truth. It cannot be explained. Truth cannot be acquired. Truth is that which is discovered. ★★

How can you see the kingdom of God in all the manifestation?

If you develop your eyes to see, you can see it. For instance, what man thinks, he sees. All man sees is his own thought. Man can produce out of his thought a ghost, Satan or a saint, and he can produce out of his thought God, the most Merciful and Compassionate. Man's thought has great power, and when he has come to the realization that all is from one source and all is developing towards one goal, then he begins to see that this goal is God, and in all things he begins to see that goal. Then the world of variety is no longer variety to him: it is unity, it is one.

Do plants and animals, and mountains and streams have an apparent individual existence in the higher planes, as human souls do?

★ See Appendix, page 186, on God's Justice.
★★ Continued on page 195. Appendix on Reincarnation.

MANIFESTATION OR THE MANIFESTED SOUL

All that exists in the lower plane has its existence in the higher planes also. The word individual is itself a puzzle. Every thing and being which stands distinctly separate may be called an entity. But what we call individual is a conception in our imagination, and the truth of that conception is realized on the day when the ultimate truth will throw its light upon life. Then one will no more speak about individual. One will say 'God', and no more.

There are beings, but there is One Being; there are many, but there is only One. Therefore, if one asks; 'Are all objects, such as plants, animals, streams and mountains living beings?' Yes, it is true: they are all living beings. 'Have they a separate existence?' Yes, but only to our outer vision. If our inner vision is open, the separateness is gone. Then there is one vision and that is the single immanence of God.

What happens to animals such as dogs when they die? Do they retain their individuality?

Yes, they retain their individuality until they reach a certain point.

Is it true that animals have a group soul? Not each a soul?

That is a conception of some people. There is one, and there are many. These two things must be understood. In the manifestation there are many; in truth there is one. For instance, there is the rise and fall of a nation, and there is the prosperity and decline of a race, and so there is also the birth and death of a world.

Yet, along with all these group souls, we are all individual entities; and so are the animals. At the same time we are one; we become one as a race, as the whole world. In this sense, if a person wishes to make a speculation on the animals having a group soul, he may. But in point of fact, every animal, tree or plant has its own soul and spirit. They may call it

79

by a different name – see it in the form of a group soul, as France as a nation has its good and bad qualities. That is another thing. If we admit that the animals have a group soul, then we must admit that human beings have a group soul also. Neither by speculating on this do we produce a new doctrine or spirit, nor by not admitting it do we show greater wisdom. Both points of view are right. We can be a group, and we can be separate – as our body is a group, and yet every part is a separate thing. If the hand is hurt, one separate thing has been hurt. If we go into this matter more deeply, we shall find a wonderful phenomenon working through life; we shall come to a place where the whole nature of being will unveil itself, and we shall be able to see nothing but God.

CHAPTER 16

28th August, 1923, 5.30 p.m.

THE soul which has already brought with it from the angelic heavens a luminous body, and from the sphere of the *djinns* a body full of impressions, functions in the end in the human body which the physical plane offers it, and it settles for some time in this abode. This completes what we understand by the word individuality. These three planes are the principal planes of existence[32]. The human being, therefore, has all three beings in him: the angel, the *djinn* and man.

What man acquires on the earth is the experience which he gains by the means of his senses, an experience which he himself gains; it is this experience which man collects in that accommodation within himself which he calls the heart. After this is collected he calls that surface of the heart, which is the collection of his knowledge, mind. This word comes from the Sanskrit *manas*, which means mind, and from this the word 'man' has come.

The question arises: 'How far does man recollect the memory of the angelic world and of the *djinn* world?' Man shows the memory of the angelic heavens and the sphere of the *djinn* by his tendencies. His tendency towards light, truth, love and righteousness, his love of God, his seeking for the truth of life, this all shows the angel in him. His longing for beauty, his drawing towards art, his love for music, his appreciation of poetry, his tendency to produce, to create, to express, all this shows the signs of the *djinn* sphere in him. And the impressions which constitute his being, which he has brought as a heritage from the sphere of the *djinn* which have been imparted to him by the souls on their way back to the goal he shows also as something peculiar, and different from what his family possesses.

No doubt it often happens that a child possesses qualities of his ancestors which were perhaps missing in his parents, or even two or three generations back. However, this is another heritage, a heritage which is known to us as such. I might express this by saying that the soul borrows a property: a property from the spheres of the *djinn*, and a more concrete property from the physical world. And as it borrows this property, together with this transaction it takes upon itself the taxation and the obligations as well as the responsibilities which are attached to the property. Very often the property is not in proper repair, damage has been done to it, and it falls to his lot to repair it; if there be a mortgage on that property, that becomes his portion. Together with the property he becomes the owner of the records and the contracts, and all the papers of the property he owns. In this is to be found the secret of what is called *karmā*.

What makes the soul know of its own existence? Something with which it adorns itself, something which it adopts, possesses, owns and uses. For instance, what makes a king know that he is a king? His palace, his kingly environment, people standing before him in attendance. If all that were absent, the soul would be no king. Therefore the king *is* a palace. It is the consciousness of the environment which makes the soul feel, 'I am so and so'. What it adorns itself with makes it say, 'I am this or that'. Otherwise, by origin, it is something nameless, formless. On the earth plane the personality develops out of the individuality. The soul is an individual from the moment it is born upon the earth in the worldly sense of the word, but it becomes a person as it grows. For personality is the development of individuality, and in personality, which is formed by character building[33], is born that spirit which is the re-birth of the soul.

The first birth is the birth of man, the second birth is the birth of God.

Is there any likeness between the angelic body, the *djinn* body and the physical body of a person?

No definite design of that likeness may be made, but they are all developing towards the image of man, which is – as is said in the Scriptures – made after the image of God. What may be said is only this: that the physical body is the most distinct and clear, the *djinn* body is less distinct, more phantom-like, and the body of the angel is still less distinct, but only less distinct to the physical eyes. So one cannot make comparisons between the beings of the earth and of the other spheres. If there is any similarity, it is because the whole manifestation is a development towards the human image. This truth can be found even in the study of natural science and biology.

Are the differences of the rays going to the different kingdoms differences in the grades of individualization?

When they start they are not marked by individualization, but as they go on they are guided and influenced at each step to take a particular direction. For instance, a child was born; on growing up he went to see a play; he liked it so much that he became an artist – that was the second thing. It means that one step helps another step. In this way the soul's direction is changed.

Are those differences of evolution of the soul produced by differences of time? A soul which is more individualized, did it come from God a longer time ago?

No, it has nothing to do with time. It is according to the strength, the Light and the volume of the ray that the individuality is more concrete and more perfect. The older soul is the grown-up soul, the one which has absorbed the wisdom before it came to this plane. It depends on the impression it got from the *djinn* world; it depends on the properties it has.

If it has nothing to do with time, does that mean that time does not exist?

Yes, time does not exist. But here it means that the attraction from the soul toward its body of manifestation has nothing to do with time. In the angelic world there is distinction of three kinds: of volume, of radiance of the Light, and of shortness and longness of life. In the *djinn* world comes the attraction to the form; from there evolution is different. The attraction to the form is from the *djinn* world. If, for instance, a man is a thief, that is because he became a thief in the *djinn* world; there he was impressed by theft.

But what makes a soul impressed by one thing and not by another?

Its grade of evolution, its volume and its Light.

Does the individuality end, or does it improve?

It improves.

Does a soul travel up and down from the one plane to the other plane, and back again.

Yes, this is true. But from a spiritual point of view it is not true, for the soul does not travel: the soul is always in God. Soul itself is God. Instead of saying that the soul travels, we can rightly say that God travels. Travelling means losing consciousness in one plane and awakening in another plane; but the soul does not travel, the soul remains in God. Though the individuality begins from the divine Spirit, the oneness is so great that – although we cannot say it is the same soul – we can say it is the same I-ness.

Also, it is not the soul which reincarnates, it is the soul that gains and loses consciousness on the different planes. It is the vehicle of consciousness on the different planes which reincarnates. The whole puzzle is solved by solving the question: who is 'I'? 'I' is God Himself.★

CHAPTER 17

29th August, 1923, 5.30 p.m.

THE law that governs the soul's manifestation may be divided into three parts: that of the angelic heavens, that of the sphere of the *djinn*, that of the world of man or the physical plane.

In the angelic heavens there are no distinct impressions, but there is a tuning. The soul is tuned to a certain pitch by the law of vibration, high or low, according to the impressions it receives from the souls coming back home. In this tuning it gets, so to speak, a tone and rhythm which direct its path towards the world of the *djinn*. Souls in themselves are not different in the angelic heaven, as it is immediately next to the divine Being. If there is a difference of souls in the angelic heaven, it is the difference of more or less radiance, and a longer or shorter scope of their range.

That which attracts souls from the sphere of the *djinns* to the human world, is what they receive from the souls who are homeward bound.[34] In accordance with this they take their direction towards the physical world. If I were to give this idea in a more expressive form, I would say: it is like a person whose heart is tuned to love and like things, and to appreciate and admire beauty; he will certainly take a direction towards a greater beauty, and will seek such friends to meet with and to learn from, as seem to him in some way similar to his nature or ideal. This is the example of the soul which is attracted from the angelic heavens to the sphere of the *djinn*. A person who has studied music and practised through his life will certainly seek the association of musical friends, artists, singers, composers and lovers of music. Among these he will find his friends, his comrades; and so a soul from the sphere of the *djinn* is directed, according to its love for certain things, to find those things on the physical plane.[35]

★This answer is continued in Appendix, page 189, on The Destroying of the Past. See also Appendix, page 191, on Reincarnation.

MANIFESTATION OR THE MANIFESTED SOUL

This shows that God does not thrust certain conditions upon the souls going to manifestation, but in this manner they choose them. A person may say: 'But no soul can have chosen miserable conditions for itself! How then do some souls happen to be born in miserable conditions?'[36] The answer to this we find before us in this world. Many here cause their own miseries. They may not know it, they may not admit it, nevertheless many of men's joys and sorrows are caused by themselves. I do not mean to say that this is the only law that governs life. No, this is a law which answers the question that arises out of common sense. But if one raised one's head from this world of illusion and looked up and asked God: 'Tell me the secret and the mystery of Thy creation', one would hear in answer that every thing and being is put in its place, and each is busy carrying out that work which has to be done in this whole scheme of nature.

Life is a symphony and the actions of every person in this symphony is the playing of his part, his particular part, in this music. When the war was going on, all people were called to arms and were placed where they were needed, regardless of their profession, qualifications or moral standard. The reason was that the call of the purpose was to be the first consideration. If there is anything which will bring peace to the thinker, it is the understanding of this. The thought: 'I am suffering now because of my sins in a past life', may bring an answer to the enquiring and reasoning mind, and stop it from rebelling for the moment. But will this take away the irritation that the misery is causing in the heart? Will that mind ever excuse God for having so severely judged him? He will own his mistakes of the past, but will he ever believe in God as a God of love and compassion, as a God of kindness and mercy, and as a God of forgiveness?

> You said that the sum total of every person's difficulties is the same. For what period of life did you mean this? For one earthly life, or for the time during the journey towards manifestation?
>
> What we can call the sum total is the horizon; but if we have to point out which is the horizon and where is the horizon, we cannot do so, and as we go toward the horizon, we find the cause and effect

diminishing, becoming paler and paler, and summing up into one life.

The farther we reach, the closer we come to that equilibrium which is shown by the sign of the serpent with the tail in its mouth. Neither is there tail, nor is there mouth. Mouth and tail are, so long as the serpent is straight. Mouth and tail are no longer, as soon as the serpent has curled itself and put its tail in its mouth. Then wisdom is perfected.

For instance, there was a man who once hated his neighbour. He quarrelled and fought with him and took revenge. There were fights and quarrels, they exchanged ill-will. In the end the heart of the person was melted, and he said: 'What are we quarrelling about? It is just a misunderstanding of one word I have said. I am sorry.' The whole thing which was built into a mountain dropped, the whole world of hatred crumbled from that moment, nothing of the past was left. They became friends and loved one another.

There comes a moment – and that moment is every moment, and as we go on so there come moments – when things sum up. It is the finishing of them, they are no longer. The farther we go, the more things finish. All our disputes and arguments about differences and distinctions, and about high and low, good and bad, all pale and fade away as we go farther. They become so faded away, that no colour is left in them. Then that white light comes, which is the Light of God. It is that attainment which Buddha has called *nirvāna*, which means: no colour. What is colour? What is green, what is blue, what is high and what low, what is better and what worse, what is right or wrong, sin or virtue? All this is colour. All colours for our common sense become a property, a reality, but in the realm of truth they fade away, they have no existence.

He who realizes this has entered *nirvāna*. *Nirvāna* is not an intellectual realization, it must be lived. If someone runs away with your hat, you run after him and he says: 'It is mine, it is not yours!' That is the test, whether he has the *nirvāna*. But there are blessed souls, the souls who are really satisfied when they see another person eating his dinner. There are such souls living on earth to-day who, on seeing another person adorned in beautiful clothes, are satisfied. Their gladness is to see another person dressed beautifully. We might think: 'What a renunciation, what a self denial!' It is not so. They have risen above it. They have gone through a cross, and they arrive at *nirvāna*. In such a stage sacrifice gives them no pain, it only gives them pleasure.

The spark of this *nirvāna* is in every soul. *Nirvāna* is the perfection of that, but the spark is in every soul. The other day I said to a child: 'Would you rather give your toy to the other child, who is poor?' Now this child had just got its toy and had not yet played with it. I saw the face of the child and said: 'Would you really be glad to see another child playing with your toy? You should not give it, if you were not glad'. And I tell you, it was just striking a match to kindle that spark of *nirvana* hidden in every soul, which was in the heart of the child. The child went at once and gave its toy, and you should have seen the face of that child. It was beaming with joy at the happiness of giving it. It was happy to think that the other child was happy. There was no end to its happiness.

So *nirvāna* is not something which we must learn by study, and we need not torture ourselves to learn it. It is in us, but it becomes buried in us. If it was only dug up by our love for it! We need not look for it, it is not something which we acquire. *Nirvāna* is a star in our heart which will develop and as we develop it, so it becomes brilliant and its brilliancy consumes all the impurities of life. Call it sin, or wrong, or mistake of the past, it eats it all up and turns it all into purity, which is the divine Light.

What is the significance of the word *nirvāna*?

The word *nirvāna* means: no *vāna*, which means no

difference, no distinction. When one has risen above difference and distinction, that is *nirvāna*.

CHAPTER 18

31st August, 1923, 5.30 p.m.

THE soul comes on earth rich or poor, ripened or unripened, through three phases where it is either enriched or has lost its opportunity. It takes Light from the angelic heavens, knowledge from the sphere of the *djinn*, and it inherits qualities from its parents and ancestors on the earth plane. Of these things that it has collected on its way to its manifestation on the earth, it has made that accommodation which is called the mind. The body in which the soul functions on the physical plane also contributes to the soul the properties of all the worlds to which it has belonged: of the mineral kingdom, the vegetable kingdom and the animal kingdom. It is for this reason that man is called a universe in himself, for man consists in himself of all that is in heaven and all that is on the earth. 'We have made him Our *khalīfah*, says God in the Qur' an referring to man, meaning: Our representative, Our chief, into whose care a universe is given.

Man verily is himself the universe.

Man shows in his life the traces of all the conditions through which the clay that makes his body has gone. There are atoms of his body which represent the mineral kingdom, the vegetable kingdom, and the animal kingdom; all these are represented in him. Not only his body, but his mind shows the reflection of all the kingdoms through which his body has passed, for the mind is the medium between heaven and earth. Man experiences heaven when conscious of his soul. He experiences the earth when conscious of his body. Man experiences that plane which is between heaven and earth when he is conscious of his mind. Man shows by his stupidity the mineral kingdom which is in him, thick and hard. Man shows by his pliability the vegetable kingdom in him, by his productive and creative faculties which bring forth the flowers and fruits of his life from his thoughts and deeds. Man shows the traces of the animal kingdom in him by his passions, emotions and attachment, by his willingness for service and usefulness. And if one were to ask, 'what represents the human in him?' the answer is: all things, all the attributes of earth and heaven. The stillness, hardness and strength of the stone, the fruitfulness and usefulness of the vegetable kingdom, the fighting nature, the tendency to attachment from the animals, the inventive, artistic, poetical and musical genius of the sphere of the *djinn*, the beauty and illumination, love, calm and peace of the angelic planes, all these things put together make man. It is therefore that the human soul consists of all and thus culminates in that purpose for which the whole creation has taken place.

Does the soul find the accommodation of the mind when it arrives on earth, or does it make it afterwards?

The soul brings on earth an accommodation, already made in a very negative state, from the world of the *djinns*. That is the place where it gets the mould of its mind. But that accommodation is filled later on after the soul's wakening on the earth plane. It is here that this accommodation completes itself and becomes mind.

Is it only a mould?

Yes, first it is only a mould with impressions; that is the accommodation. For instance, there is one child who very attentively hears music. There is another child who runs away from it, his mind has not got that mould, music is not engraved there. He will learn it, as he will hear it. But the child who has already that mould is musical. He will seek music to come and fit in that mould which is already there.

Can you explain what makes some souls unable to progress, as if they were dead?

I should think it is the reflection of the mineral kingdom. Thickness is the only convenient word I can find. For instance, if the sun is thickly clouded, the light does not reach the earth. So the soul, which is divine and has all the Light, if it is thickly clouded, then man does not receive the Light which is in himself. The Light is there, but he does not receive it. Diamonds allow themselves to be cut, human nature does not.

What difference is there between a diamond and an ordinary stone? The difference of thickness. The diamond reflects the light which falls upon it, and the stone is so thick that it will not allow the light to reflect itself in it. The diamond allows the light of the sun to reflect itself in it; the stone does not.*

CHAPTER 19

1st September, 1923, 5.30 p.m.

THE soul manifested on the earth is not at all disconnected with the higher spheres. It lives in all spheres, but knows mostly one sphere, ignorant of the others on which it turns its back. Thus the soul becomes deprived of the heavenly bliss, and conscious of the troubles and limitations of life on the earth. It is not true that Adam was put out of the Garden of Eden, he only turned his back on it, and it was like an exile from heaven. The souls of seers, saints, masters and prophets are conscious of the different spheres. It is therefore that they are connected with the worlds of the angels and *djinns* and with the Spirit of God. The condition of the former** becomes like that of a captive who is imprisoned on the ground floor of the house and has no access to the other floors of the building, and that of the latter*** is that he has access to all the different floors of the building, wherever he may wish to dwell.

The secret of life is that every soul by its nature is *asmān* or *ākāsha*, an accommodation, and has in it an appetite. Of all that it partakes, it creates a cover which surrounds it as a shell, and the life of that shell becomes dependent upon the same

*This answer is continued in Appendix, page 199 on Responsiveness and Discipleship.
**i.e. the soul which turns its back on the higher sphere.
***i.e. the soul of the seer, saint, master and prophet.

substance of which it is made. Therefore the soul becomes susceptible to all influences and subject to the laws of that sphere from which it seeks its sustenance, which means the sustenance of the shell[37]. The soul cannot see itself; it sees what is around it; it sees that in which it functions; and so it enjoys the comforts of the shell which is around it, and experiences the pains and discomforts which belong to the shell. In this way it becomes an exile from the land of its birth, the Being of God which is the divine Spirit, and it seeks consciously or unconsciously once again the happiness and peace of home. God therefore is not the goal, but the abode of the soul, its real Self, its true being.

There are five spheres of which the soul is capable of being conscious. What are these spheres? These spheres are the different shells, each shell having its own world.

The first sphere of which man becomes conscious after his birth on earth is *Nāsūt*, a sphere which is commonly known as the physical plane. How are the comforts and discomforts of this plane experienced? Through the medium of the physical body. And when there is something wrong with an organ of the body or of the senses, the soul becomes deprived of that particular experience that it would like to have on this physical plane. The physical body, susceptible to all changes of climate, becomes dependent in its experience and expression, thus making the soul dependent and limited. Therefore, with all the riches that the world can give, man – who is only conscious of this sphere – is limited.

'God alone is rich, and all souls living on earth are poor.' (Qur'an)

Malakūt is the next sphere, the sphere of thought and imagination, where there is greater freedom and less limitation than one experiences on the physical plane. A man with thought and imagination can add to life that comfort and beauty which is lacking on the physical plane; the more real the imagination becomes, the more conscious of that sphere of mind he proves to be. This sphere of mind is his world, not smaller than this world but much larger, a world which can accommodate all that the universe holds – and still there would be a place to be filled.

Then there is a third sphere, *Jabarūt*, a sphere of the soul, in which the soul is at home. In the waking state the soul of the average man only touches this sphere for a moment at a time. Man does not know where he is at that moment. He calls it abstraction. Do they not say, when a person is not listening, that he is not here? Every soul is lifted up to that sphere, even if it be for only a moment, and by the life and Light with which the soul is charged in that sphere, the soul is enabled to live on this earth the life full of struggles and difficulties. Nothing in the world could give man the strength that is needed to live a life on the earth if there were no blessing from heaven reaching him from time to time, of which he is so little aware.

The other two spheres are experienced in sleep, but they are not different spheres; they are only different because they are experienced in sleep. They are *Malakūt*, which is experienced in dreams, the world of mind, of thought and imagination; and *Jabarūt*, the state of deep slumber, when even the mind is still; a sleep which makes suffering patients free from pain and prisoners free from their prison;[38] that state of sleep which takes away from the mind its load of worries and anxieties, and removes from the body every exhaustion and tiredness, bringing to mind and body repose, rest and peace, so that, after man has wakened from his deep sleep, he feels comfortable, rested and invigorated, as if a new life had come to him. One would give anything in the world to have a deep sleep, though so few of us know its value.

That state of *Malakūt* is reached while in the waking state by the great thinkers, the great inventive minds, by the gifted artists, and it is experienced by the seers and sages. It is to experience this that all the concentrations are given by spiritual teachers to the adepts. This fuller experience is then called *Lahūt*.

Still another experience is *Hāhūt*, a further stage which is experienced by souls who have attained the highest spiritual attainment, which is called *Samādhi* in Vedantic terms. In this experience a person is conscious of *Jabarūt* while awake, and this state he brings about at will.

Though for the sake of convenience these spheres are explained as five spheres, yet chiefly they are three: *Nāsūt*, the plane of the world of man; *Malakūt*, the sphere of the *djinn* and *Jabarūt*, the angelic world.

Now there is the question if a soul, by rising to all these spheres, becomes conscious of the sphere of the *djinn* and of the

angelic heavens, or if it only sees its self-made world of mind
and the spheres of joy and peace within itself. The answer is:
first it sees its own world. By rising to the sphere called
Malakūt it experiences the joy and peace which belong to its
own heart and which are of its own being. But that is one part
of spiritual attainment. This part of attainment is the way of
the Yogi. That in which the Sufi differs from the Yogi is his
expansion. It is these two sides of the journey which are
pictured by the two lines of the cross: the perpendicular and
the horizontal. The perpendicular line shows a progress
straight within, from *Nāsūt* to *Jabarūt* experiencing one's own
world, one's self within. But that which the horizontal line
denotes is expansion. The Sufi therefore tries to expand as he
goes on progressing, for it is the largeness of the soul which
will accommodate all experiences and in the end will become
God-conscious and all-embracing.

The man who shuts himself up from all men, however high
spiritually he may be, will not be free in *Malakūt*, in the higher
sphere. He will have a wall around him, keeping away the
djinns, and even the angels when in the angelic heavens. So his
journey will be exclusive. It is therefore that Sufism not only
teaches concentration and meditation, which helps one to
make one-sided progress, but the love of God, which is
expansion, the opening of the heart to all beings, which is the
way of Christ and the sign of the cross.*

CHAPTER 20

3rd September, 1923, 5.30 p.m.

[39]THERE arises a question: 'What is the cause of the different
stages of evolution that one sees in the world of variety?' The
answer is that there are three principal causes: first, the heritage
of the soul, which it has brought from the angelic and from the
djinn worlds; second, the inherited qualities that a soul
possesses, having received them from its parents and

* See also Appendix, page 200 on The Soul's Journey, Appendix, page
202 on Meditation and Appendix, page 205 on the Sufi and the Yogi.

ancestors; and third, what the soul acquires after coming on earth. It is these three things which make what may be called individuality, which in its result culminates in a personality.

There are five principal stages of evolution recognized by the Sufis, named as five conditions of *nafs*, the ego. Every condition of the ego shows its pitch of evolution. As there are five elements and five notes recognized by the ancient musicians, so there are five egos, each showing a certain pitch.

Ammārah is the condition of ego when it is blinded by passions. This shows the animal in man, and it is its fullness which is meant by the word devil. Man, absorbed in his passions and emotions, is a kind of drunken person. He cannot always see the right, the right way in thinking, saying, or doing. No doubt there are moments when every drunken person is sober, when he realizes his follies; but very often the longing to be intoxicated again sounds louder in his head, above the soft murmuring of his follies.

The second, *Lawwāmah*, is the condition of mind which is full of thoughts, good and bad, over which the ego reigns, self covering the truth. He has bitterness or spite against another; or has ways of getting all he desires cleverly; or he finds fault with others. He is worried about himself, anxious over his affairs, troubled about unimportant things; he struggles along through life, being confused by life itself. It is not that his passions and emotions trouble him; what troubles him is his own thoughts and his feelings.

Then there is a third, *Mutma'innah*, the person who, after his troubles and struggles through life, has arrived at a certain state of balance, of tranquillity; having arrived at this stage, he is beginning to enjoy to some degree the happiness which is within. He then concerns himself little with others for his own happiness; he then troubles little with others for their faults; he then knows how to throw off from himself the load of anxieties and worries that life in the world puts upon one's shoulders; he is then able to harmonize with others, to agree with others, and thus he brings the harmony within himself in his own atmosphere, and spreads it around and about him, thus harmonizing the whole atmosphere.

The fourth is *Salīmah*, who has arrived at a point where, though he be in the midst of the life of the world, he can yet rise above it. So life does not trouble him as much as it can trouble others. To him life is of no importance, yet he fulfils his obligations, his duties in the world in the same way as everybody else. He is the one of whom it may be said that he is in the world, but is not of the world. His love embraces every soul that seeks refuge under his influence. His peace stills the mind of all he meets, regulating it to the same rhythm as his own. When the soul has arrived at this point, he becomes a blessing to himself and to others.

And there is the fifth, *'Alīmah*, or God-conscious. His language becomes different; you cannot understand what his 'no' means, what his 'yes' means; you cannot very well comprehend the meaning of his smiles or of his tears. He may be sitting before you, but he is not there; he may be speaking with you and yet communicating somewhere else; he may be among all and yet absent. You may think you hold him, but he is not there. It is this soul which proves the fulfilling of that purpose for which it came on earth.

The soul has not come on earth to die the death of helplessness, or continually to suffer pain and misery; the soul has not come on earth to remain all through life perplexed and deluded. The purpose of the soul is that for which the whole creation has been busied, and the fulfilling of that purpose it is, which is called God-consciousness.

Can you explain further what causes these differences?

There are many mechanical reasons. For instance, if a person is bad natured, it is because he has acquired that nature, or because his position makes him so, or because people make him so. There is also another reason: because something is wrong with him physically, though no one knows it. A person is ill; at that time he will be irritable. A person is tired; at that time he will be disagreeable. The reason is a mechanical, physical reason, not a moral reason.

There is another reason which can be seen from another point of view, which is the difference of vibrations. Every soul that starts from the divine Sun vibrates differently. What makes the notes of the piano different? Their difference of vibrations. Only when they are harmonious they give us great pleasure. So the vibrations with which these souls start from the angelic world are of various kinds. That is the beginning, and those vibrations harmonize and co-ordinate all that comes in harmony with them.

In this way, by a vibratory law, the souls attract and harmonize first the equal vibrations. For instance, a person comes into the room, a stranger. You feel like welcoming that person, like talking to him. There is something attracting you to him. Another person comes into the room, he repels, his personality is repellent even before he has spoken one word. What is the cause? It is the vibrations. When they do not harmonize with a person, that person feels a chill in his soul; he feels it even physically and mentally. His nerves cannot stand the presence; he wants to run away.

The souls which have started from the angelic plane are nothing but vibrations. In the Christian Scriptures it is spoken of the angels playing the harp. They have no earthly harps, they are vibrations; and therefore, in accordance with their note of harmony, they attract what first comes to them and what harmonizes with them; and they are directed to that, because they are living vibrations; they are life itself.

When the soul comes to the angelic plane, is there already a tendency to differ?

According to their own vibrations they harmonize with those souls which are of the same harmony. There are different laws of harmony which I have given in 'The Mysticism of Sound'. I shall tell in short of two different kinds.

The first law of vibration and of harmony is that the similar element attracts the similar kind. This means that a conceited person will become attracted to a conceited person, a humble person will be attracted to a humble person. So good is attracted to good, and bad to bad. It is just like the note C on the piano. If you play the note C on the piano in six or seven octaves, it will sound harmoniously, because it is the same note. Wherever there is the same note, there is attraction.

There is another law, the law of contrast. That law of contrast is such that sixty will be attracted to forty in order to make one hundred, and ninety-nine will be attracted to one in order to make it complete. What one lacks, something completes it, and that attracts. Very often it happens that, although what one lacks may have very little value in comparison with what one has, yet one will pay anything to have what one lacks. That is the law of contrast. So you will always find that people will say, 'Why does a serious person seek friendship with a childish person?' That is what he lacks! All day with a long face, what must he do? He must have something to give the other side. It will benefit him; it will complete his life.

At the beginning the difference of vibrations may seem unjust. But if everyone vibrated in the same way, there would be no harmony?

Rumi says: 'Suppose we find the cause behind every cause, where shall we end?' Is there any cause, or are there endless causes? There should be some end. The end is God, and when we come to that end, there is no cause. God is the cause. That is the inspiration of the prophets. They give the causes which are, perhaps, useful for the nourishment of the intellect, but at the same time they say that the cause of all causes is one Cause, and that is God.

CHAPTER 21
4th September, 1923, 5.30 p.m.

EVERY person shows from his earthly heritage a nature that divides men into four classes.

The first is that of the idealist, who lives in the world for his ideal and with his ideal. A man of principles, intelligent, modest, moderate in everything, patient, a man with manner, dreamy by nature or a deep thinker, a man of dignity, who guards his reputation as one would take care of a thin glass. His contact with the earth is like that of a bird in the air which builds its nest upon a tree, descends to the earth to pick up a grain when hungry, then flies off, even frightened with the flutter of leaves. He lives on the earth because he is born on the earth, but in reality he lives in his thoughts. The earth and all that belongs to the earth is his need, not his want.

The second class is that of the artist, an artist not necessarily by profession, but by nature; artistic by temperament. This man shows choice in his love, he is distinct in his likes and dislikes, subtle, clever, witty, observing conventions and yet not bound by them; one who notices everything and yet does not show himself fully; elusive by nature, yet tender and affectionate, fine and simple, sociable and yet detached. He shows a likeness to a deer in the woods, who is one moment in one part of the forest and at another quite a distance away. One may think that by coming into contact with him one has got him, but at the next moment one will find him far away from one's reach. This is the type of man of whom one might say: 'I cannot understand him'.

The third is the material man, material in his outlook, devoid of the love of beauty, concerned only with all he needs, clever, but not wise. He lives all through life in the pursuit of earthly gains, ignorant of the beauty life can offer, looking from day to day with hope to that gain towards which he is working. In connection with this man one might say that he is waiting for the day when his ship will arrive.

The fourth is a man with all mundane desires, who enjoys his food and drink. What he knows is his bodily comfort, his momentary pleasures, his passing joys; the slave of his passions and captive to the things of the earth. He is simple, uninterested in everything but himself. He belongs to no one, nor does anyone in reality belong to him. He is happy-go-lucky by nature, yet susceptible to depression and despair. It is in his case that one might say that he lives to eat.

These four different qualities belong to the body that the earth offers to the soul; the third and fourth qualities more than the first and second. It is thus that one can trace back the origin of this clay that the soul has donned and called 'myself'; this clay that has passed through so many different conditions while being kneaded: through the mineral, vegetable and animal kingdoms, and then of which was made the image of man.

Verily in man is reflected all that is on earth and in heaven.

> Will you please tell us, if you include the mind in this inherited body? Is not idealism in the mind more than in the body?

Yes, it is so, but at the same time the body could be so mundane that it could stand against idealism, if it did not allow the mind to express itself fully. It should be the body that is pliable to the ideal.

> All souls start from the angelic plane pure of faults, because there is no impurity and wickedness and all is perfection, is it not so?

It is not so. There is purity, there is no wickedness, but there is no perfection. There is only one perfection and that is in God. There cannot be perfection where there is duality. Where there is 'two' there is no perfection, there is only a glimpse of perfection. God also is perfect, when He rises above 'one'. Even 'one' limits Him.

> Is it then on earth that the soul learns all the imperfections which every human being shows?

Imperfection is not learned. Imperfection is a state of being. It is limitation which is imperfection. Limitation is the condition of life. If God is perfect, all others are imperfect. However great, virtuous, pure, strong, mighty, they are all imperfect. All goes towards perfection. This whole manifestation is made so that we all may go towards perfection. The interest of life is going towards perfection. If we were born perfect, there would be no joy in life, no interest. The whole beauty we enjoy in life is from our imperfection that grows to perfection. We admire something which is greater than we are. If there was nothing to look up to, there would be no purpose to live for. Therefore one must not make too great haste in spiritual attainment. It is bad to be too impatient.

Is it possible to change one's class as one improves?

All is subject to change. One could change entirely from one type to another. Yes, even with such a vast distance as there is between saint and sinner, one can be changed into the other.

I am always unwilling to admit wickedness when I am told 'this person behaved very wickedly last month.' If that person is brought to me, I will say, 'Last month is too far, that is gone, it may not be so to-day. Even if he were wicked yesterday, to-day he may be different, there is hope for him. An accusation of last month has no claim for me to-day.'

The reason is that man by nature is good. Goodness is his very self, his very being. Badness is only a cloud over him, and a cloud is not such a thing which is pinned; it is ever floating, it is sometimes here, sometimes removed. Do clouds remain in the same position? So badness, evil, does not remain. It is just a cloud that passes, it comes and goes. If we trust in the goodness of man, there may be a thousand clouds of wickedness, they may disappear in one day. Our very trust will disperse them, for the depth of every soul is good. It is belief in this doctrine which can be the reason for the belief in the goodness of God. God cannot be good, if man can always be wicked, for the origin of man is in God. As God is good, so man is good. Wickedness is a passing phase.

Will you please tell us what determines the choice of the four qualities that the earth offers to the soul?

Really speaking, these distinct qualities are also a speculation of the human mind, as the human mind distinguishes these four qualities; but in point of fact there are millions of qualities. Every quality has its origin in the heritage, and it is a kind of mixture of different qualities, a kind of solution, just like a medicine is made of different drugs and herbs. And as one prescription is not like another prescription, so every person has a peculiar personality, has his peculiar qualities, unlike others;

Every person is unique in his way, and in this lies the secret of the oneness of God. Not only is God One, but man is one, unlike anyone else. In this God proves that He is One.

Then everyone has everything in him, but in different degrees?

Yes, and at the same time it is not necessary to be discouraged or disappointed in life, because man has the key of his own life in his hand, if he only knew it! It is absurd to say, 'I have not got this.' There is nothing in this world that man has not got, either a good quality or a bad quality. Man has got everything in this world and his denying having it makes him weak and ignorant of the key he has.

The greatest psychological secret is this: what one thinks desirable, what attracts, one must affirm and say one has it in oneself; and what is undesirable one must deny, one must say, 'It does not belong to me'. That is the key.

THE BODY

CHAPTER 22

2nd July, 1923, 5.30 p.m.

THE word *ākāsha* in the language of the Hindus is expressive of a meaning that explains its object. *Akāsha* means accommodation – not necessarily the sky,[2] although the sky is an accommodation – and on the model of *ākāsha* the whole creation has been based.

The organs of the senses – the ears, the eyes, the nostrils, the mouth – all are different aspects of *ākāsha*, and in the same way the human body is constructed. The purpose of this construction can be found in its own nature. As the purpose of the ears is found in hearing, of the nostrils in breathing, of the eyes in seeing, so is the purpose of the whole body. The purpose of the body is to experience life fully. The body becomes a vehicle for the Intelligence, through which it is enabled to experience life fully.

In order to make sound more audible people build domes and other places where resonance is produced and the voice and word are made clearer. So the construction of the body is made to make all that is perceptible clear, for by nature the body is the vehicle of the Intelligence or of the soul, through which it experiences life fully[40]. But as man has lived for generations a life of increasing artificiality, he has moved farther and farther from nature. Therefore this vehicle which was made a perfect instrument to experience life fully, has become more and more incapable of attaining that object. It is this incapability of experiencing life fully, and the innate desire for experience of life, which makes the soul strive for spiritual attainment. What man does not know, he thinks does not exist. In this is to be found the reason for materialism. But the tendency towards spiritual realization remains there as an innate desire which is consciously or unconsciously felt by every soul, whether spiritual or material. It is for this reason that a material person has a silent craving in his heart to probe the depths of the spiritual ideal which he disowns.

MANIFESTATION OR THE MANIFESTED SOUL

The work of the senses is to experience taste, smell and touch, to hear and to see. Besides these senses, there is the inner sense which is one sense. It is by experiencing through different organs of the senses that the one sense becomes many senses. It is the same sense that hears, sees, smells, tastes, and feels touch, but because it experiences life through different organs, man divides the one sense into five senses. The depth of that sense which is the inner sense is more subtle that one can imagine. When that sense finds a free expression, it not only experiences life more keenly through the organs of the senses, but it becomes independent of the organs of the senses. It penetrates through life deeply and – as Kabir says – 'it sees without eyes and hears without ears'.[41] The reason is this: all that exists is contained in an accommodation, in the ākāsha, and by being in the ākāsha the nature of all things is revealing. Plainly speaking, there is nothing in this world that does not speak. Every thing and every being is continually calling out its nature, its character and its secret. The more the inner sense is open, the more it becomes capable of hearing the voice of all things.

In every person this sense is for the greater part hidden, buried, and its being buried gives it a discomfort, for it is something which is living, the only living being there is. The idea of the Lost Word[42] has its secret in this. When once this inner sense has broken the walls around it which keep it closed, it breathes freedom, and the soul attains that happiness which is the soul's own property.

Every discomfort, from whatever source it comes, comes through the lack of understanding. The more the inner sense is covered, the more the soul finds itself in ,obscurity. It is therefore that the sign of the enlightened soul is readiness to understand. For that reason these souls are easy to conciliate. When a person himself understands better, he can make another person understand better also; but when a person is himself perplexed, instead of making another person understand, he confuses him. In this way differences are produced.

CHAPTER 23

3rd July, 1923, 5.30 p.m.

THE organs of the senses are the *ākāshas* or accommodations, of grosser and finer nature. The finer the organ, the more perception it has. Grossness takes away from the organ its power of perception. This shows that the body may be likened to a glass house made of mirrors. In the Persian language the poets have called it *ā'ina khāna*, meaning the temple of mirrors. The eye stands as a mirror before all that is visible, it reflects all that it sees. The ears are the accommodation for the re-echo of every sound that falls upon them. In other words, they are the mirror of every sound. The senses of touch and of taste are grosser compared to the senses of sight and hearing; at the same time their nature is the same. All the different sweet, sour and salt savours, and the feeling of warmth and cold are perceived by them, and they stand as mirrors in which taste and touch are reflected. Therefore, as one sees oneself reflected in the mirror, so this body stands as a mirror in which every experience of the outer life is reflected and made clear. If the mirror is dusty, it does not reflect the image clearly; so the experience of life is not clear, when the body is not looked after according to the spiritual point of view.

The Sufis say that the body is the temple of God, but the right interpretation of this saying would be that the body is made to be the temple of God. A temple cannot be called a temple of God, if God is not brought and placed there. So it is natural, when a soul feels downhearted or depressed, that there is something wrong with the vehicle. When the writer wishes to work and the pen is not in order, it annoys him. There is nothing the matter with the writer, it is the pen which is not right. No discomfort comes from the soul. The soul is happy by nature, the soul is happiness itself. It becomes unhappy when something is the matter with its vehicle, which is its instrument, its tool, with which to experience life. Care of the body, therefore, is the first and the most important principle of religion. Piety, without this thought, is of little significance.

The soul manifests in this world in order that it may experience the different phases of manifestation and yet may not lose its way and be lost, but may attain its original freedom – in addition to the experience and knowledge it has gained in this world. The different exercises that the Sufis and Yogis do in order to enable the mind and body to experience life more fully, exercises such as fasting, pose and posture, movement, all these help to train the body, that it may become a fitting vehicle for the experience of life.

Wonder working, such as psychometry, feeling the atmosphere of places, of objects, of people, all this comes when the body is also prepared for it. A person may be intelligent, clever, learned, good or pious, and yet his sense of perception may not be fully awake. It must be remembered as the first principle of life that manifestation was destined for keener observation of life within and without.

Is every unhappiness a material phenomenon?

The greatest unhappiness that a person feels is from lack of mastery. The unhappiness comes when, knowing of mastery, he yet cannot practise that which he knows. Sadness comes from limitation, limitation in different forms: lack of perception, lack of power upon oneself or upon conditions, or from the lack of that substance which is happiness itself, which is love.

If a person has mastery, is he not still unhappy by the unhappiness of others?

There is often lack of understanding, though there may be love; and often lack of love through lack of understanding. There may be love and understanding and yet lack of power. Unhappiness comes always from limitation.

Can there be love without understanding?

If love has reached perfection, it will attain all power. When love becomes power, love becomes understanding. The nature of love is as the nature of water hidden in the depth of the earth. If one does not dig deep enough one finds mud, not water; but when one digs deep enough, one finds water. Many lovers of God lose patience, trust and hope. They have touched mud and not reached water. But when they have dug deep enough they find pure water.

If a person can be happy by the power of his soul, this means that he can wipe out his sins. But how is it with the debt he has to pay sooner or later?

There is a board, and the board comes to an end after a hundred years; it wears out gradually. But if you know how to end it, you may put it in the fire and finish it in one moment. Or, by surrounding it with some chemical substance, you may preserve it for a very long time. So it is with sins; all that has been made, can be destroyed.★ If one individual has the power of destroying, another has the power of creating. Creating is more difficult than destroying.

A great Sufi saint said, on hearing his mureeds discussing problems of sin and virtue, reward and punishment: 'My murīds★★, do not worry over problems of sin and virtue. They are things which man makes'. The difficulty is that man lives so much in the outer life. He thinks he can destroy a table or a chair, because he can hold them in his hands; but what he holds in thought and feeling, he is not master but slave of. If he can learn to be master of his thoughts and feelings, he can destroy what he wishes.

CHAPTER 24

4th July, 1923, 5.30 p.m.

As there are different organs of sense, so there are the centres of inner perception. These centres are the seats of the intuitive faculties. Two among these centres are of great importance: the heart and the head. If the Sufi training differs from that of the Yogis, it is in training both these centres together, by

★ See Appendix, page 189 on 'Destroying the Past'.
★★ murīd: one who is desirous to learn, pupil, disciple.

which the Sufi produces balance. The head without the heart shows dry intellect, the heart without the head represents an unbalanced condition. Balance is the use of both these faculties. The whole Sufi training is based upon this principle.

The centres may be likened to the space that one finds in the apple. They are an *ākāsha*, an accommodation, where not only scent, touch, hearing and sight are perceived, but even the thought and feeling of another; the condition in the atmosphere, the pleasure and displeasure of one's fellowman are perceived, and if the sense of perception is keener, then even past, present and future can be perceived. When man does not perceive in this way, it does not mean that it is foreign to his nature; it only means that the soul has not developed that power of perception in his body. The absence of such finer perception naturally causes depression and confusion, for the soul longs for a keener perception and feels confused, and at times agitated, owing to the lack of a fuller perception – as a person who is blind feels nervous, because the inner longing is to see, and when the organ of sight fails him, he becomes agitated.

This is generally the hidden cause in many souls who feel restless. Life, as we live it, is a life of artificiality, it works against it★. We need not read the ancient traditions to find out the truth about it. To-day, in people who live a less artificial life, a more simple life, a life in and near nature, the intuitive faculties are keener, and these people show a greater happiness.

These centres become blocked by certain foods and by living a more materialistic life. These centres are located in certain places, and as there are some plants in the caves of the mountains where the sun does not reach and the air does not touch, and it is difficult for the plants to live there, so are the centres of perception located in the physical body. The body is nourished by food, but these centres remain without any nourishment. The physical body which is made of matter, its sustenance is matter; but the centres of perception are of still finer matter, and though they are located in the physical body no nourishment can reach them, except that which is drawn through the breath, the fine substance which is not even

★ i.e. against fuller perception.

visible. In the language of the mystics it is called *nūr* which means light.

The body not only wants food, but also breath, in other words vibration; and that vibration is given to it by the repetition of sacred words. The sounds, the vowels and the composition of the sacred words are chemical and it is this chemistry which was called by the ancient philosophers alchemia. These centres are the *ākāshas* or domes, where every sound has its re-echo; and the re-echo once produced in this *ākāsha* or *asmān* reaches all other *asmāns* which exist within and without. Therefore the repetition of a sacred word has not only to do with oneself and one's life, but it spreads and rises higher than we can imagine, and wider than man can perceive.

Verily, every action sets in movement every atom of the universe.

What do you mean by saying that breath gives food and breath to the centres?

Food and breath both. Food taken into the breath, and breath also in a symbolical sense: breath created by the power of vibration. Just as in an engine steam is necessary as well as the engineer, so in the working of the centres two things are necessary: nourishment of finer food inhaled through the breath, and vibrations of finer motions created by the repetition of a certain word. Those words set certain atoms in motion, so the centres come into life again.

What is the value of the sacred words?

The mind has its own vibrations. For instance, a person in a chaotic state of mind comes into your presence, and you feel it at once. Therefore thought has its vibrations, but thought and word together make the vibration more perfect, more powerful.

Would people live longer than they do, if conditions were better?

There have been times when men lived much longer than now. Life is not meant to be painful, and yet in human life one experiences pain in everything: pain in birth, pain in death. It should not be, it comes from artificial life, from an unnatural state of living. Man has gone far beyond the normal state of living.

Will you tell us more about the Sufi training and that of the Yogis?

See Appendix, page 205 on 'The Sufi and the Yogi'.

CHAPTER 25

6th July, 1923, 5.30 p.m.

WHEN once the inner sense has become keen, it shows its development first by working through the organs of the senses. The vision becomes clearer, the hearing becomes clearer, the sense of touch is felt more keenly, the senses of taste and smell become clearer. Therefore, among those who tread the mystic path, one finds many who are sensitive and become more sensitive as they develop spiritually. As the standard of normal health known by the average person is much beneath the mystical ideal, often to the uninitiated the sensitiveness of a person of mystical temperament may seem peculiar. At the same time when it is developed by spiritual training, the sensitiveness is under control. This manifests as the first thing in the life of a seer. The body which covers the soul keeps it blind by depriving it of its freedom of expression in keener perception[43]. It is like a captivity for the soul. When the centres in the body are awakened and at work, then the soul experiences life more keenly, and naturally clouds which give depression clear away. The soul begins to look forward to life with hope and trust and with courage, and thus attains that power and understanding which is needed to struggle through life.

When a little more advanced, the Intelligence begins to see through the eyes what every eye cannot see; the finer forces of nature manifest in colours and forms. There are many who talk much about this and some who know but say little, for they do not see wisdom in speaking about something which the person standing next to them does not see. Among those who speak much about seeing many things which others do not see, there is hardly one who really sees. There is no doubt, as the sight becomes keen, first the finer colours of different elements working in nature manifest to the view. Next the atmosphere that is created around man, which is composed of semi material atoms, becomes manifest to the eyes. This is what is called the *aura*. The different colours of the same denote the meaning, for there is nothing is this world which is without meaning. The one who pursues the meaning of life in all its aspects hears again in the end the Word which was once lost for him.[42]

No doubt, the life of a sensitive person becomes difficult, especially when one has to live amidst the crowd. It is for this reason that the Brahmans lived an exclusive life, which has been criticized by some who do not know the meaning of it. Different practices of breathing become a great help in training both mind and body to make them more perceptive, in order that they may become fitting vehicles to fulfil the purpose of life.

THE MIND

CHAPTER 26

8th July, 1923, 5.30 p.m.

THE mind is made after the body; it is therefore that its form is that of the body. We read in the Old Testament that the heavens were made after the earth. The real place where the heavens are made is within man. The mind is made of all one learns, one experiences, one loves and one remembers. It is therefore that man is that which his mind contains. If his mind contains a sorrow, man is sorrowful. If his mind contains joy, he is joyous. If it contains success, he is successful. If it contains failure, failure awaits him, everywhere he moves he finds failure. The mind is an accommodation in which man collects all that he learns and experiences in life.

In short, man is his mind. How true therefore the claim of the dervishes when, sitting on the bare earth, clad in rags, they address one another: 'O King of Kings, O Monarch of Monarchs!'. That is their usual way of addressing one another. Their voice is the voice of true democracy, for this claim of theirs is the expression of their being conscious of the kingdom of God.

The mind is not only the treasure house of all one learns, but it is creative by nature. The mind improvises upon what it learns, and creates not only in imagination, but finishes its task when the imagination becomes materialized[44]. The heavens and the infernal regions – both – are the creations of the mind and both are experienced in the mind.

The question: 'Is the body not born with a mind, did the mind not exist before the body?' may be answered: yes, it did exist; it existed as an *ākāsha*, an accommodation. And the question, 'Was this accommodation formed on any certain model or design?' – may be answered thus: the first design of this *ākāsha* is moulded upon the impression that falls deeply upon the soul, the soul coming towards manifestation from the infinite Spirit. If we picture the infinite Spirit as the sun, the soul is as its ray. The nature of the soul is to gather on its way

111

all that it can gather, all that it happens to gather, and to make a mould out of it.

It is this impression that has helped to form the first mould of the mind. It manifests its original nature and character through the body with which it is connected and identified. The impression of the nature and character of the parents, of the ancestry, of the nation and race, follows after the first impression that the soul has taken on its way. If this happens to be the impression of one personality having fallen upon the mind going towards manifestation, in the life of that person the distinct characteristics of a certain personality who has lived in the past will show clearly. It is in this that the secret of the doctrine of reincarnation which the Hindus have held can be recognized.★

There are souls which come from the infinite to the finite existence and there are spirits★★ which return from the finite existence to the infinite; their meeting ground is on the way. It may be one impression, or it may be several impressions which help to mould this *ākāsha* which, after it is once connected with the body, becomes the mind. For the mind is not complete until it is filled with the knowledge and experience the soul gains by the help of the physical body.[45]

The question: 'Those who leave the body and pass away from the earth, is their mind not complete without the body?' may be answered by saying that their mind is already completed by the experiences made in their life on earth through the medium of the physical body.

> Is the mind complete when people die very young?
>
> The mind is complete according to the experience it has. Then you can call it mind. As long as the mind is not formed, the soul has not become individualized. It is not the body by which it becomes individualized, it is the mind by which it becomes individualized, through the medium of the body. The mind as a record begins as soon as the child sees and hears.

★ See Appendix, page 197 on 'Reincarnation'.
★★ Souls returning from the physical plane are called spirits. Cf. page 24.

Does the soul retain the experiences gained on earth?

This question brings one to the ultimate truth. You see, the light in all its forms is the light of the sun; in the gas, in the electric light, in the candle, in the star and the planet, it is all the property of the sun, but we call it by different names. The soul is the life and the light itself, it is God's own Being. It manifests outwardly, and because of the smallness of the channels through which it comes, it becomes small. But it is larger than we can possibly imagine. When the light is put out, it is not lost, for it is the property of the sun.

Every experience, even of animals, of germs, all is collected and all remains in the one Mind which is the Mind of God, distributed at the same time to different souls. The closer we are to this Mind, the more we benefit; and so we all have the right to make use of the storehouse of God. Therefore spiritual persons have been inspired physiciens, scientists, kings, judges, inventors, statesmen, because they got the key to the storehouse of knowledge. Scientists, such as Edison, may not appear to be spiritual, but their soul touched the storehouse of knowledge and they got inspiration. Solomon said: 'There is nothing new under the sun'. All the knowledge that ever was, is stored in the storehouse of God and can be gained in accordance with our openness. [46]

Can an illuminated soul be conscious of all the past events in the evolution of man?

To some extent; for I would ask: 'This eye which is so accommodating, does it collect within itself all that it sees? And the mind, by which man has got the most wonderful source of record, the memory, does it always remember all that it sees and experiences through life?' No, only certain things which have made a deeper impression upon it. If we remembered all the faces we have seen after a trip to Paris, I don't know where we should be! And if we remembered all things, all the books we have read, all the good and bad words people have said, insults and bitterness and foolish and crazy things, where should we be at the end? The human being, his mind, his body, and his health, all depend on what he takes in and what he puts out. If it were not so, he could not live. He takes in the essence and throws the refuse away. Therefore, from the angelic world and from the *djinn* world – if one takes something – it is the essence, the essence of one's experience. If this were not so, how could man live with such numberless impressions weighing on his mind? How could he digest?

But there is another thing. I think that person is not to be complimented who remembers every good and bad thing of the past. He ought to be pitied, for he must have a great many experiences of great remorse, which would only create bitterness in him. It is the greatest relief to forget. It is like bathing in the Ganges; the meaning of which is: to be purified of the past. The present has so many beautiful things to offer us – if we only open our eyes to look at them – that we do not need to look for beauty in the past. Beauty is always there, we only have to open our heart to look at it – ever new, ever fresh.

Does the soul come on earth many times?

It is very difficult to define 'soul'. The best answer is: the soul is the ray of the Sun, which is the infinite Spirit. The ray is an action of the Sun, which is the ray itself. It manifests and returns, just as man inhales and exhales. Man's breath is himself. The existence is of the One Whose action it is. So is the soul we speak of.

MANIFESTATION OR THE MANIFESTED SOUL

CHAPTER 27

7th July, 1923, 5.30 p.m.

THE mind is not necessarily the brain. The mind is a capacity, an *ākāsha*, which contains all the experiences we have in life. It has all the impressions we gain through our five senses. It is not only within the body, but also around the body; but the centres of perception reflect every thought and feeling and thus man feels that the mind is within him. In point of fact the body is within the mind and the mind within the body[47]. As the eye sees an object before it and reflects it, so the centres of perception reflect every thought and feeling. For instance, the sensation of joy and depression man feels in the centre called the solar plexus; this does not mean that joy or depression is there, but that this centre is sensitive to such experiences.

The mind for the sake of convenience may be called a substance which is not necessarily matter, but a substance quite different from matter in its nature and character. There are objects which give more resonance to sound and there are other objects which respond less to sound: sonorous objects such as metals of different kinds, which reproduce sound clearly, and then stone and solid wood, which do not respond to sound. Such is the difference between mind and body.

The mind is a better vehicle for the intelligence than the body. Therefore, though the mind experiences life even through the material organs of the senses, still the mind itself is more perceptive and can experience life in its different aspects, standing apart from the body. In other words, the mind can see for itself and it can hear, even without the eyes and the ears, for the mind has its own eyes and ears. Though the mind needs the physical eyes and ears to see and to hear with, still there are things which the physical eyes cannot see, the physical ears cannot hear. The mind sees and hears these. The more independent the mind is made of the outer senses, the more freely it perceives life, and the more it becomes capable of using the outer senses, the organs of the senses, to their best advantage.

The question: 'Has the mind a form?' may be answered: yes,

the mind has the same form as the form with which the soul is most impressed. The question: 'What is the form with which the soul is most impressed?' may be answered: one's own form. That is why, when man says 'I', he identifies himself with the form which is most impressed upon his mind, and that is his own.

But the mind is a world within itself, a magic world, a world which, compared with the physical form, can be more easily changed, more quickly altered. The phenomenon of the mind is so great, and such wonders could be performed if only one had the key to the mind in one's hand! The difficulty is that man becomes so fixed in his physical body that he hardly realizes in his life that he has a mind. What man knows of himself is of the body, though the mind which is called *manas* in Sanskrit is at the root of the word man.

Verily, man is his own mind.

What is the key to the mind?

The key to the mind is to open the house of the mind, to open all the doors and cupboards and see what is hidden, what is valuable, what is worth while keeping and what should be put out.

The soul is like the crown prince. He does not know the secrets of his kingdom. He knows he is the crown prince, and once he has got the key, he enters into possession of it. His kingdom is there before him.

What is the relation between mind and brain?

Brain is the receptacle of mind; brain reflects mind. But where is the brain? Is it in the head? Not necessarily. The head is the seat of the brain, but the brain is all over the body. Therefore it is not only the head which reflects the mind, but the whole body.

Is the form of the mind character?

No, the form of the mind is what the mind thinks about, and it thinks generally about the body which is attached to it. So when anything is wrong with the body, the mind feels, 'I am ill'. While the pain and discomfort is in the body and not in the mind, it is reflected back in the mind. The mind has power to hold everything in its memory. So if the body is cured through medicine, and the mind still holds the thought of pain, the body cannot give up the illness.

The greatest difficulty in the spiritual path is to remove the false self from the intelligence. It stands in the way of the soul, it strives for all that pertains to the false self. So the soul is kept busy with something which in the end is nothing, and it cannot see beyond.

CHAPTER 28

10th July, 1923, 5.30 p.m.

THE mind is not only the *ākāsha*, which contains all that one learns and experiences through life, but among the five different aspects of the mind – each having its own work[48] – there is one aspect which may be especially called the mind, and which shows the power of the creator. All that we see before our eyes and all the objects made by the skill of man, every condition brought about in life, whether favourable or unfavourable, all are the creation of the human mind; of one mind or of many minds.

Man's failures in life, together with the impression of limitation which he has, keep him ignorant of that great power which is hidden in the mind. Man's life is the phenomenon of his mind. Man's happiness and success, man's sorrow and failures are mostly brought about by his own mind, of which he knows so little. If this secret had been known by all, no person in this world would have been unhappy, no soul would have had failure, for unhappiness and failure both are unnatural. The natural thing is to have all man wants and wishes. No doubt, first one must know what one wants and the next question is, how to get it. The words of Emerson[49] support this argument: 'Beware of what you want, for you will get it'. The whole of life is one continual learning, and for the one who really learns from life, the knowledge is never enough. The more he learns, the more there is to learn. The

117

secret of this idea★ is in the Qur'an: 'Be' – He said – and it became.' The seers and knowers of life do not only know this in theory; it is their life's own experience.

There is a story told among Hindus about a magic tree[50]. A man was travelling in the hot sun toward the woods. He became so tired that he felt like sitting under the shade of a tree. Then he thought: 'If there were a little mattress to sit on, it would be better than to sit on these hard stones!' And as he looked, he saw the mattress already there. Then he thought the tree was so hard to lean against, and when he turned, he saw there was already a cushion. Then he thought: 'This mattress is too hard. If only I had another cushion to sit on, now that I am so tired!' and it was there. Then he thought: 'If I had some cooling water, some syrup, that would be very nice!' and he saw someone bringing him the syrup. He was astonished and very glad. Then he thought: 'This tree is not sufficient to sit under. A beautiful house would suit me!' and a beautiful little house was there. Then he thought: 'Walking in the woods is very tiring; I must have a chariot!' and the chariot with the horses was there. After this he became very astonished and could not understand. He thought: 'Is all this true, or is it only my imagination?' Then everything disappeared; only the hard stones remained and the tree above them. That is the story of the mind.

The mind has the power of creating. It creates everything. Out of what does it create? Out of mazing *māyā*[51], a substance subject to change, death, destruction. However, the power of the mind is beyond question. Does this not teach us that mostly our unhappiness and failures are caused by our own mind more than by the mind of another? If caused by the mind of another, then our mind is not in working order!

The knowledge of the power of mind is then worth knowing, when the moral conception of life is understood better, when man knows what is right and what is wrong, what is good and what is evil, when he judges himself only, and sees these two opposite things in his own life, person and character. For man sees the folly of another and wishes to judge another, when his sense of justice is not wide awake.

★i.e. that man's life is the phenomenon of his mind.

MANIFESTATION OR THE MANIFESTED SOUL

Those whose personality has brought comfort and healing to their fellowmen were the ones who mostly used the faculty of justice to judge themselves; who tried to correct themselves of their own follies, and being engaged in correcting themselves, had hardly time in life to judge another. The teaching of Christ: 'Judge ye not, lest ye be judged', will always prove the greatest example to be followed.

The mind is a magic shell, a shell in which a design is made by the imagination, and the same imagination is materialized on the surface. Then the question: 'Why does not all we think come true? – why is not all we wish realized?' may be answered that by our limitedness we, so to speak, bury the divine creative power in our mind. Life confuses us so much, that there is hardly one among a thousand persons, who really knows what he wants; perhaps among a million there is one who knows why he wants it; and even among many millions you will not find one with the knowledge why he should want it and why he should not want it.

With all the power of the mind, one thing must be remembered: that man proposes and God disposes. This will always prove true when man's desire stands against the will of God Almighty. Therefore the path of the saints in life has been to seek with resignation the will of God, and in this way to swim with the great tide so that, with the accomplishment of their wish, the purpose of God may be fulfilled.

> Do you mean to say that the key to the mind is the wish for morality? In other words, that it lies in the heart?

The key to the mind is the knowledge of life. There is only one real knowledge. It is learned in one moment, if one remembers; but the nature of life is such that we forget.

The key to the mind is the knowledge of life. In other words, it is the psychology of life, and very rarely is there a person who knows the psychology of life profoundly. Man has the faculty for knowing, but he is so absorbed in life that he does not give time to learn the psychology of life, which is more precious than anything in the world.

I mean by psychology that before uttering a word

a man thinks what effect it might have on the atmosphere, on the person, on the whole life. Every word is a materialization of thought, it has a dynamic power. If one considered, one would find that every little thought, every little feeling, every little movement one makes – even a little smile or a little frown, such a small thing – has its effect. If one knew the effect of every cause before bringing that cause into thought, speech or action, one would become wise. Generally man does all mechanically, influenced by the conditions of the time: 'Anger or downheartedness did it. He did not do it, but his broken spirit did it.' So every man in life lives a life without control, in other words, without mastery.

What we learn in spiritual knowledge is to gain mastery, to learn what consequences our actions will bring. A man cannot be perfect in this knowledge; all souls have their limitations, but it is something to strive after. In this is the fulfilment of God's purpose. Even this knowledge alone does not make man capable; practice is necessary, and practice may take a whole life. Every day one seems to make more mistakes. This is not really so, but one's sight becomes keener.

What of those who do not think of all this? Every change of mood or emotion changes their actions, words and thoughts, and so they can never accomplish the thing they have come to accomplish. All their life is passed in failure and mistakes, and in the end they have what they have made. So it is always true that life is an opportunity. Every moment of life is valuable. If one is able to handle oneself, one has accomplished a great deal.

CHAPTER 29
11th July, 1923, 5.30 p.m.

THE mind has five different aspects, which are distinguished as the different departments of the mind, which have their own work to do. First, the heart which feels and which contains in itself four other aspects of mind. Second, the mind which creates thought and imagination. Third, memory. Fourth, the will which holds the thought. Fifth, the ego, that conception of mind which claims to be 'I'.

There is no mind without body, for the body is the vehicle of the mind. Also it is made by the mind, not by the same mind but by other minds. The child not only inherits the form and feature of his parents and ancestors, but their nature and character, in other words their minds which mould its mind and body.

The mind is not only the creator of thought, but it is a receptacle of all that falls upon it. The awakened mind makes the body sensitive to all different feelings; the sleeping mind makes the body dull. At the same time the fineness of the body has its influence in making the mind finer, and the denseness of the body makes the mind dense. Therefore mind and body act and react upon one another. When there is harmony between the mind and body, health is secure and affairs will come right. It is the disharmony between mind and body which most often causes sickness and makes affairs go wrong. When the body goes south and the mind north, then the soul is pulled asunder; then there is no happiness. The secret of mysticism therefore is to feel, think, speak and act at the same time, for then all that is said or felt or done becomes perfect.

The different minds in the world may be likened to various mirrors, capable of projecting reflections, and subject to reflecting all that falls upon them. No one, however great in wisdom and power, can claim to be free from influences. It is like the mirror claiming, 'I do not reflect all that falls upon me.' Only the difference between the wise and the foolish is that the wise turns his back on what he must not reflect; the foolish not only reflects the undesirable thought, but most proudly owns it.

The mind is creative and the mind is destructive; it has both powers. No thought ever born of the mind, be it even for a second, is lost. Thought has its birth and death, as has a living being, and the life of the thought is incomparably longer than that of the living beings in the physical body. The relation of the thought – which is created by a certain mind – to that mind is that of the child to its parents. It is therefore that man is not only responsible for his actions, but even for his thoughts. Souls would become frightened if they had a glimpse of the record of the thoughts they have created, without meaning to create them, under the spell of their ever changing moods. As the Prophet said: 'This life of the world which once was so attractive will one day appear before them as a horrible witch. They will fly from it and will cry, "Peace, peace!"'

It would not be an exaggeration if one called the mind a world: it is the world that man makes, in which he will make his life in the hereafter, as a spider weaves its web in which to live. Once a person thinks of this problem he begins to see the value of the spiritual path, the path in which the soul is trained not to be owned by the mind, but to own it; not to become a slave of the mind, but to master it.

What is meant by 'feeling, thinking, speaking and acting at the same time?'

It means that all our activities are devoted to one direction, and this concentration of every form into one action has the perfect power.

Is thought only killed or finished by another thought?

Yes. A kind thought will kill a cruel thought. Man remains always like a child, something of childishness always remains. To be really grown-up is the ripening, and when the mind is not ripened, it is raw, unripe. That troubles others, because fruit was created to become sweet and to give pleasure and happiness. So does a ripe personality; if a person does not become ripe the purpose of life is not fulfilled.

Many people say, 'I don't mind how I act in life or what people think.' Then there is no fulfilment of life. The fulfilment of life's purpose is to mind: not to mind others, but to mind ourselves. If we knew what to mind, we would only mind ourselves.

Can illness be produced through the fault of others? Or are we always at fault when we are ill?

Man is always at fault, at a thousand faults. Illness can have several causes: inharmony between the mind and the body, inharmony in life. Illness is inharmony. If one will avoid inharmony, one will be well. This is the key to life.

The first thing is to make peace with oneself, and that gives the strength of a thousand. If one falls down by trying to do good to others, one has done no good to others. But if someone was so strong that he could stand alone, that would be good work. The idea is this: we must first be concerned with ourselves, make our thought, word and action harmonious; then we give an example, and this must sooner or later have its effect. There is no use troubling about others. We must try to correct ourselves, because there is no end to the corrections we need in everything. An awakened soul does not concern himself with the faults of others, but is concerned with himself and takes himself to task.

Has life in the hereafter development and the opportunity to go onward?

Yes, for the mind is creative. It retains its creative tendency all through, here and in the hereafter. Since the mind is creative, it is progressive, and so there is opportunity to progress here, and also in the hereafter.

What is the meaning of your words, 'There is no mind without a body', and, 'The body is made by the mind, not by the same mind but by other minds'?

This means: the mind before the body was made, was only an *ākāsha*. The experience it has gained through the body as its vehicle has become its knowledge and it is this knowledge which makes

123

the *ākāsha* mind. The *ākāsha* which becomes mind, after the body has been born on earth, has already gathered some indistinct knowledge from several minds, with which it came in contact while coming to the earth. Perhaps it gathered more from one mind than from other minds. In that case it has gained more characteristics of one individual who has passed from the earth. Upon that knowledge this *ākāsha* has gained, through the parents, the knowledge or the mentality of their ancestry, of their nation, of their race, and of the particular grade of evolution of that time of the whole humanity.

THE SOUL

CHAPTER 30

1st August, 1923, 3.30 p.m.

IT has been asked of the sages and thinkers of all times, by the seekers after truth, that they should explain the meaning of the word soul. Some have tried to explain it, and some have given answers which may be difficult for everyone to understand. About the meaning of the word soul many statements of thinkers differ, although all mystics arrive at the same understanding of the idea of the soul.

As the air being caught in the water becomes a bubble for a moment, and as the waves of the air being caught in a hollow vessel become a sound, so Intelligence being caught by the mind and body becomes the soul. Therefore Intelligence and soul are not two things; it is only a condition of the Intelligence which is the soul. The Intelligence in its original aspect is the essence of life, the Spirit, or God. But when this Intelligence is caught in an accommodation such as body and mind, its original nature of knowing then knows and that knowing Intelligence becomes consciousness. The difference between consciousness and the soul is that the soul is like a mirror, and the consciousness is a mirror which shows a reflection in it.[52]

The Arabic word *rūḥ* and the Sanskrit word *ātmā* mean the same thing: soul. There is another word: 'sole' in the English language which means one or single. Although different in spelling it is yet expressive of the same idea, namely that the soul is that part of our being in which we realize ourselves to be one single being. When one thinks of the body, it has many organs. When one thinks of the mind, it has various thoughts. When one thinks of the heart, it has many feelings. But when one thinks of the soul in the right sense of the word, it is one single being; it is above division. Therefore it is the soul which really can be called the individual. Very often philosophers have used this name for the body, mind and consciousness, all three.

Sufism originally comes from the word *safā*[53], which means purity. This purity is attained by purifying the soul from all foreign attributes that it has acquired, thereby discovering the real nature and character of the soul. Pure water means something which is in its original element. If it happens that there is sugar and milk in the water, then the one who wishes to analyse it will separate the elements and will try to see the water in its pure condition. Sufism therefore is the analysing of the self, the self which has for the moment become a mixture of three things: body, mind and soul. By separating the two outer garments of the soul the Sufi discovers the real nature and character of the soul, and in this discovery lies the secret of the whole life.

Rumi has said in the 'Mathnavi' that life on earth is a captivity of the soul. When one looks at the bubble in which the air has been caught by the water, one sees the meaning of Rumi's words: that something which is free to move about, becomes captive by the atoms of water for a time, and loses its freedom for that moment.

Man in all conditions of life, whatever his rank, position or possessions, has troubles, pains and difficulties. Where do these come from? From his limitations. But if limitation was natural, why should he not be contented with his troubles? He is not contented, because limitation is not natural to the soul. The soul who is by nature free, feels uncomfortable in the life of limitation in spite of all that this world can offer. When the soul experiences the highest degree of pain, it refuses all that this world can offer to it in order to fly from the spheres of the earth; it seeks the spheres of liberty the freedom of which is the soul's predisposition. There is a longing hidden beneath all the other longings man has, and that longing is for freedom. This longing is sometimes satisfied by walking in the solitude, in the woods; when one is left to be by oneself for a time; when one is fast asleep, when even dreams do not trouble one; and when one is in meditation in which, for a moment, the activity of both body and mind is suspended. Therefore the sages have preferred solitude, and have always shown love for nature; they have adopted meditation as the method of attaining that goal which is the freedom of the soul.*

* See Appendix, page 202 on Meditation.

CHAPTER 31

1st August, 1923, 5.30 p.m.

$Dh\bar{a}t^{54}$, the primal Intelligence, becomes captive to knowledge. That which is its sustenance limits it, reduces it, and pain and pleasure, birth and death are experienced by the Intelligence in this captivity which we call life. Death in point of fact does not belong to the soul, and so it does not belong to the person. Death comes to what the person knows, not to the person. Life lives, death dies. But the mind which has not probed the depths of the secret of life becomes perplexed and unhappy over the idea of death. A person once went to a Sufi and asked him what happened after death. He said: 'Ask this question of someone who will die – of some mortal being, which I am not.'

Intelligence is not only a knowing faculty, but is creative at the same time. The whole of manifestation is the creation of the Intelligence. Time and space both are nothing but the knowledge of the Intelligence. The Intelligence confined to this knowledge becomes limited, but when it becomes free from all knowledge, then it experiences its own essence, its own being. It is this which the Sufi calls the process of unlearning, which purifies or makes the Intelligence free from knowledge. It is the glimpses of this experience which are called ecstasy, for then the Intelligence has an independent joy which is the true happiness. The soul's happiness is in itself, nothing can make the soul fully happy but self – realization.

The phenomenon which the Intelligence creates by its creative power becomes a source of its own delusion, and as the spider is caught in its own web, so the soul becomes imprisoned in all it has created. This picture we see in the lives of individuals and of the multitude. Motive gives power and at the same time it is motive which limits power, for the power of the soul is greater than any motive; but it is the consciousness of the motive which stimulates the power and yet robs it of its power. The Hindus have called the whole phenomenon of life by the name $m\bar{a}y\bar{a}^{51}$, which means puzzle; and once the true nature and character of this puzzle is realized, the meaning of every word of language becomes untrue, except one: 'truth', which words cannot explain.

Therefore the soul may be considered to be a condition of God, a condition which makes the Only Being limited for a time. The experience gained in this time with its ever changing joy and pain is interesting, and the fuller the experience the wider becomes the vision of life. What one has to experience in life is its true being. The life which everyone knows is this momentary period of the soul's captivity; beyond this man knows nothing. Therefore every change that takes place he calls death or decay. Once the soul has risen above this illusive phase of life by climbing on to the top of all that is besides itself, it experiences in the end that happiness for which this whole creation took place.

The uncovering of the soul is the discovering of God.

The word intelligence, as it is known by us and spoken of in everyday language, does not give a full idea; especially the word intelligence, as used by modern science, will only convey to us something which is the outcome of matter or energy. But, according to the mystic, Intelligence is the primal element or the cause as well as the effect. While science acknowledges it as the effect, the mystic sees in it the cause.

One will question: 'How can Intelligence create this dense earth which is matter? There must be energy behind it?' But this question comes, because we separate Intelligence from energy or matter. In point of fact, it is spirit which is matter and matter which is spirit. The denseness of spirit is matter, and the fineness of matter is spirit. Intelligence becomes intelligible by turning into denseness. That denseness, being manifest to its own view, creates two objects*: *Dhāt*, the Self and *Ṣifat*[55], what is known by the Self; then comes of necessity a third object, the medium by which the Self knows what It knows: *Naẓar*, the Sight or the Mind. The Sufi poets have pictured these three in their verse as *Bāgh*, *Bahār*, and *Bulbul*, the garden, the spring and the nightingale.** It is these three aspects of life which are at the root of the idea of the Trinity. The moment these three are realized as one, life's purpose is fulfilled.

*i.e. establishes the dual aspect.
**Symbols used in the Persian mystic poetry.

MANIFESTATION OR THE MANIFESTED SOUL

As matter evolves, so it shows intelligence, and when one studies the growing evolution of the material world, one will find that at each step of evolution the material world has shown itself to be more intelligent, reaching its height in the human race. But this outcome of the development of matter is only the predisposition of what we call matter, which is manifested in the end. Everything in nature is the evidence of this truth. Even in the vegetable world we see that the seed which is at the root of the plant is also its result. Therefore, it is the Intelligence which comes as the effect, and the very effect is the cause.[56]

Does motive limit the intensity of power as well as its width?

Certainly. Motive is a shadow upon the Intelligence. It might seem that it increases the power, but no doubt at the end one finds out that it robs the power.

However, the higher the motive, the higher the soul; the greater the motive, the greater the person. When the motive is beneath one's ideal, then it is the fall of man, and when the motive is his ideal, it is his rise. According to the width of motive man's vision is wide, and according to the power of motive man's strength is great.

'WHY DO SOULS COME ON EARTH?'

CHAPTER 32

5th September, 1923, 5.30 p.m.

THE question: 'Why do souls come on earth? Why has this creation taken place? What is the purpose of this manifestation?' may be answered in one word: satisfaction, for the satisfaction of God. Why is God not satisfied without it? Because God is the Only Being, and the nature of being is to become conscious of being. This consciousness experiences life through various channels, names and forms; in man this consciousness of being reaches its culmination. Plainly speaking, through man God experiences life at its highest perfection.

If anyone asked: 'Then what is man's duty, if that be the purpose?' the answer is: his sacred duty is to attain to that perfect consciousness which is his *dharma*[57], his true religion. In order to perform his duty he may have to struggle with himself, he may have to go through suffering and pain, he may have to pass many tests and trials, but by making many sacrifices and practising renunciation, he will attain that consciousness which is God-consciousness, in which resides all perfection.

But why must man suffer and sacrifice for God? At the end of his suffering and sacrifice he will find that he began to do so for God, but in the end it turned out to be all for himself. It is the foolishly selfish who is selfish, and the wisely selfish proves to be selfless.

Now comes the question: 'How may this consciousness be attained?' It is to be attained by self realization. First man must analyse himself and find out of what he is composed. He is composed of spirit and matter. He consists in himself of the mineral world, the vegetable world, the animal world, the *djinn* and the angel. It is his work to balance all these, knowing that he has neither been created to be as spiritual as an angel, nor has he been made to be as material as an animal. When he strikes the happy medium, he will certainly tread the path which is meant for a human being to tread, the path which leads straight to the goal. 'Strait is the gate, and narrow the way.' Narrow is the way, because any step taken on either side will lead to some other path.

Balance is the keynote of spiritual attainment.

In order to attain to God consciousness the first condition is to make God a reality, so that He is no longer an imagination. No sooner is the God ideal brought to life, than the worshipper of God turns into truth. There is no greater religion than truth. Then truth no longer is his seeking, then truth becomes his being, and in the light of that Absolute Truth he finds all knowledge. No question remains unanswered. That continual question that arises in the heart of man, 'Why?' then becomes non-existent, for with the rising of every 'why?' rises its answer. The moment a man has become the owner of the house, then he becomes acquainted with all there is in it. It is the stranger who finds it difficult to find any room in the house, not the one who lives in it; he knows about the whole house. What is rooted out in the quest of truth is ignorance. It is entirely removed from the heart, and the outlook becomes wide, as wide as the eye of God. Therein is born the divine Spirit, the Spirit which is called Divinity.

Is it possible for every soul to attain to God consciousness?

It is born for it. Every soul is born for it.

Is self consciousness placed higher than God consciousness in your classification?

The surface of the true self of all is God; but the depth of everyone's true self is the Self, and when I said self consciousness I meant the true Self.

That is why by God realization one realizes one's Self?

Yes.

Is it right to say that God becomes conscious of His own consciousness through man's realization?

Yes, man is the best instrument for God's own purpose. A certain satisfaction comes from having put into an objective form that which was first on another plane. It is the fulfilment of the whole life. When the gramophone was invented, what satisfaction, what exaltation it gave to the inventor! Nothing could equal this satisfaction. If anyone had said to Edison: 'You have made this new object; I will give you so much money, provided you will never hear it', he would have said: 'No, if nothing were given to me, I would rather like to hear it once'. To see how it works, that is the wonderful part of it.

The same simile can be seen in your taking parts in the Play*. You produced before me which I had once made in my mind. How could you accomplish it? You had to accomplish it by putting yourself aside. You were not yourself; you had to be different from yourself. That is the secret of the whole performance: When you are no more yourself, or what you had thought yourself to be, that is the secret.

The journey is only three steps, if one but knew how to accomplish them. Annihilation, which is such a frightening word, is nothing more than this same thing, when in the Play you came with a different name, a different form, a different appearance. It is the annihilation of the first self, of the appearance, by donning another form or appearance. But that annihilation never killed a person; it is only a change of life on the surface; it is only a continuation of life.

What are the three steps of the path of annihilation?

One step is in the ideal of form, the other step is in the ideal of name, and the third is in the nameless and formless. In Sufi terms these are called:

fanā'-fi-Shaikh – the annihilation of form.
fanā'-fi-Rasūl – the annihilation of name.
fanā'-fi-Allāh – the annihilation of both name and form.[58]

*Hazrat Inayat Khan's Play 'UNA' had been performed some days before.

PART III

The Soul Towards the Goal

(Chapters 33 – 45)

CHAPTER 33

8th September, 1923, 5.30 p.m.

THE soul during its journey towards manifestation and during its stay in any plane, whether in the heaven of the angels, the sphere of the *djinns*, or the plane of human beings, feels attraction towards its source and goal. Some souls feel more attraction than others, but there is a conscious or unconscious drawing within felt by every soul. It is the ignorant soul, ignorant of its source and goal, which fears leaving the spheres to which it has become attached. It is the soul that knows not what is beyond which is afraid to be lifted up above the ground its feet are touching. Is the fish afraid of going to the depth of the sea? But, apart from fish, even men who are born on land and have been brought up upon the land, make a practice of swimming and diving deep into the sea, and bringing up the pearl shells from the depths. There are seamen who are happier on the sea than on the land; their daring, to those unaccustomed to the phenomenon of water, is sometimes perfectly amazing.

Life is interesting in its every phase. On the journey towards manifestation as well as on the soul's return toward the goal every moment of life has its peculiar experience, one better than the other, one more valuable than another. In short, life may be said to be full of interest. Sorrow is interesting as well as joy; there is beauty in every phase of life, if only one can learn to appreciate it.

What dies? It is death that dies, not life. What then is the soul? The soul is life, it never touches death. Death is its illusion, its impression, death comes to something which it holds, not to the soul itself. The soul becomes accustomed to identify itself with the body it adopts, with the environment which surrounds it, with the names by which it is known, with its rank and possessions, which are only the outward signs that belong to the world of illusion. The soul absorbed in its childlike fancies, in things that it values and to which it gives importance, and in the beings to which it attaches itself, blinds itself by the veils of its illusion. Thus it covers its own truth with a thousand veils from its own eyes.

What is the return journey? Where does one return to? When does one return? The return begins from the time the flower has come to its full bloom, from the moment the plant has touched its summit, from the time that the object, the purpose for which a soul is born upon earth is fulfilled. For then there is nothing more to hold it, and the soul naturally draws back, as breath drawn in. But does man die by drawing in his breath? No. So the soul does not die owing to this drawing in, though apparently it gives to the dying person and to those who watch him an impression of death.

This physical body may be likened to a clock. It has its mechanism, it requires winding, and this winding keeps it going. It is the healthiness of the physical body which enables it, by its magnetic power, to hold the soul which functions in it. For some reason or other, either by disorder or by having been worn out, this body loses that power of keeping together by which it holds the soul which functions in it. It gives way, and the soul naturally departs, leaving the material body as one would throw away a coat which one no longer needs.

The connection between the body and the soul is like man's attachment to his dress. It is man's duty to keep his dress in good order, for he needs it in order to live in the world. It is ignorance, great ignorance indeed, when man forgets himself and thinks himself to be his dress! Yet so man does, as a rule. How few in this world stop to think on this subject, whether: 'this body is myself', or whether: 'my self is apart from this body, higher or greater than this body, more precious and longer living than this body'.

What then is mortality? There is no such thing as mortality, except the illusion and the impression of that illusion which man keeps before himself as fear during his lifetime, and as an impression after he has passed from this earth.

Nevertheless: 'All souls have come from God, and to Him is their return' (Qur'an).

> Would it be possible for a soul to come on earth and yet remain free from illusion and attachment?
>
> Yes, but to some extent there must be illusion and attachment; yet it can be the least attachment and illusion. If there were no illusion and attachment, it

would be like having day all the time and no night. We need day and night, both. We can enjoy the sun by having had the night. The rising and the setting of the sun, all this gives us joy and happiness. But in the illusion and attachment there is a motive power, and by that motive power a purpose in life is accomplished. If there were no attachment and illusion, even to a small extent, the soul would not be able to hold the body, because even that is attachment.

Therefore, another thing in connection with this is that there are many people who become very ill and yet do not die. For years and years they remain ill, and they do not die. The reason is the attachment to the body. As long as the attachment is there, they hold the body in a grip and the soul cannot leave it, because attachment is a soul power: the magnetism is there.

Do those, who die with an objective unaccomplished, die in a moment of despair?

It so happens, when their mind is not strong enough to hold that objective which they want to accomplish. Then it gives way. Besides that, sometimes the body is not in a fit state to hold it, and therefore one dies with the object unaccomplished.

But the object, when unaccomplished, is unaccomplished only according to the mind – not in accordance with the scheme of nature. It has been accomplished by dying a natural, peaceful death.

Do those who commit suicide out of despair, do so out of illusion?

Yes, certainly. It is just like breaking two things which are attached to one another. It is cutting them apart, soul and body, by will; separating by will soul and body which are not meant to be separated. The scheme of nature would have accomplished something, and by separating them they have deprived themselves of that privilege which the scheme of nature would have given them.

If death is not what we understood it to be, what is it?

Change. Life is change. What we call death, is our impression of that change. It is a change just the same, and if life is a change, then death is only a change of life.

What is the meaning of the Greek saying: 'Those whom the gods love die young?'

It is an exaggerated saying. It means only that even in the death of young people there is God's love. It means that there is something better for them which those on this side do not know.

CHAPTER 34

10th September, 1923, 5.30 p.m.

BOTH life and death are contrary aspects of one thing, and that is change. If there remains anything of death with the soul which has passed away from this earth, it is the impression of death according to the idea it has had of death. If the soul has had a horror of death, it carries that horror with it; if it has had agitation at the thought of death, it carries that feeling with it. Also, the dying soul carries with it the impression of the idea and the regard that those surrounding it in life had for death, especially at the time of its passing from the earth. This change paralyses every activity of the soul for some time. The soul which has become impressed by the idea that it itself held of death, and by the impression which was created by those around the deathbed, keeps itself in a state of inertia which may be called fear, horror, depression or disappointment. It takes some time for the soul to recover from this feeling of being stunned. It is this which may be called purgatory. Once the soul has recovered from this state, it again begins to progress, advancing towards its goal on the tracks which it had laid before.

The picture of this idea may be explained thus:[59] A simple man who was told in jest by a friend: 'When a person is yawning, that is the sign of death', was impressed by this idea and once, after having had the experience of yawning, he thought certainly he was dead! He was very sad over his death and went to look for a grave for himself, despairing over the thought: how false are friends, that no one came to his funeral. He found a hole in the ground dug by the wolves in the forest and he thought: 'How nice, I don't need to dig a grave for myself. At least that much is done for me.' He threw himself in that hole and lay there comfortably, sorrowing over his death. Another man happened to pass that way, who was looking for someone to carry part of his load and who was talking to himself: 'If only I had someone in these woods who would carry half my load, it would be so nice!' In answer to this thought he heard someone saying: 'Alas, now I am dead! If I were living I would certainly have helped you.' This man could not understand how a person who was dead could speak. As he turned back and looked, he found a man lazily lying in a hole dug in the ground. He thought: 'Perhaps he is ill; can I help him?' He came near and asked: 'What is the matter with you?' The simpleton said: 'Nothing is the matter with me. I am quite well, only I am dead.' The man said: 'How can you be dead and speak at the same time? You are not dead!' But the simpleton was good at argument. He still continued saying: 'No, no, I am dead.', until the man had kicked him out of that hole.

Behind this humorous story there is a wonderful secret hidden. How many souls prove simple in believing in the idea of death, carrying with them that thought while passing from the earth to a life which is still greater life. How many souls do we find in the world who believe the end of life to be death, a belief in mortality which cannot be rooted out from their minds! The whole teaching of Jesus Christ has as its central theme the unfoldment towards the realization of immortality.

> How can we make people believe in immortality and help them to rise above the fear of death?[*]
>
> It must be done gradually and not suddenly because, given suddenly, the knowledge of truth frightens a person more than death. It is therefore that the knowledge of truth was made a secret science, a

[*] Cf. Appendix, page 184 on the Fear of Death.

mysticism. Otherwise there was no need to hide it from one's fellowmen before whom one can bring anything, however precious, if it is for their good. Such is spiritual wealth. Mysticism is spiritual wealth: the more you give, the more it is increased. By giving to another soul you have not lost, only gained. What one has is doubled, when one has given it to another; but one must know whether a person is prepared.

Do you know what happens sometimes? When a person is fast asleep and you wake him suddenly, he gets a shock in his mind and body, from which he recovers with great difficulty, and which does him a great deal of harm, physically and mentally. It is the same with truth. That is the reason for all the initiations – the reason why all is secret; why, the vow of secrecy. Otherwise there is no loss in giving the truth to any soul, to friend and foe alike. A sage would be as willing to give the truth to a friend as to a foe, because once he has reached the truth there will be no longer a foe. The difficulty is that it cannot be given at once, for in the end it must prove beneficial to both. One cannot place dinner before the newborn infant, who must first be fed with milk.

How can the belief in God and the conviction of His existence be brought home to those who have none?

We must not trouble about it. We must be concerned with ourselves, because there is so much to be done with ourselves. When once God becomes reality in ourselves, then we have the living God to give to others. One person speaks of gold, the other has gold coins: he can give them. When our belief has become living, it will have influence upon others. It cannot fail, it will not fail.

Would not an unbeliever in immortality be convinced of his error by physical death?

He would be looking forward to death there, on the spiritual plane. He still has the impression that there is death. He will think, 'I am not yet dead, death will come some time and there will be an end.' The one who will not be convinced – no one can convince him, and nothing will!

Do some souls remain under the impression of death a long time?

One cannot compare the time of that world with the time of this world. The time of the next world is quite different from the time here. Certainly the length of time which they have to pass through purgatory depends upon how deep the impression was. The deeper the impression, the impression of the horror of death, the longer the time.

The sages, the prophets, have shown their spiritual advancement at the moment of their death. That is the time when the truth comes out and falseness has no chance to make a play. At the last moment, when the soul is passing from the earth, it then shows where its heart was: on the earth or in heaven; if on the earth, then its last time shows it; if in heaven, then also the last time shows it. Besides that, the person who has earned peace throughout his life, then shows his wealth when passing away peacefully, that shows his riches; and his willingness to meet with what comes in the life beyond, that shows his nobility.

Would you please tell us something about the condition of the soul when it first leaves the body?

The condition of the ordinary person is confusion, for before his death he realized that he was dying, and after death he realizes that he lives. His condition is that of a person who is still living and says: 'I am dead.' As long as this confusion remains, the soul goes no farther. It is this state which I call purgatory. When the soul has recovered itself and realizes it is still living, then the clouds of confusion are broken and the soul finds itself in the atmosphere to which it belongs.

At the moment of death is it better to fix the mind only on God, to make it blank, or else to think of religious surroundings?

140

If during life a person has trained his mind to think only of God, then it is best if he does so at the moment of death, but if he could not do this in life, he should in death think of the object of his devotion; and if he cannot do this, he should think of pleasant surroundings.

CHAPTER 35

11th September, 1923, 5.30 p.m.

WHAT is purgatory? Purgatory in Sufi terms may be called *nazā'*[60], a suspension of activity. If there is any death, it is stillness or inactivity. It is like a clock which for some time is stopped; it wants another winding and a little movement to set the clock going. So there comes the impulse of life, which – breaking through this cloud of mortality – makes the soul see the daylight after the darkness of the night. And what does the soul see in this bright daylight? It sees itself living as before, having the same name and form, yet progressing. The soul finds a greater freedom in this sphere and less limitation than it had previously experienced in its life on the earth. Before the soul now is a world, a world not strange to it but the world which it had made during its life on the earth. That which the soul had known as mind, that very mind is now to the soul a world.[61] That which the soul, while on earth, called imagination, is now before it a reality. If this world is artistic, it is the art produced by the soul. If there is absence of beauty, that is also caused by the neglect of beauty by the soul while on earth.

The picture of *jannat*, paradise, the ideas about heaven and the conception of the infernal regions is now to the soul an experience. Is the soul sent to the one or the other place, among the many who are rejoicing or suffering there for their sins? No, this is the kingdom that the soul has made while on earth, as some creatures build nests to stay in during the winter. It is the winter of the soul which is the immediate hereafter. It passes this winter in the world which it has made either agreeable or disagreeable for itself.

But one might ask: 'Do you mean to say that the soul lives a solitary life in this world that it has made?' No, how can it be solitary? The mind, the secret of which so few in the world know, this mind can be as large as the world and larger still. This mind can contain all that exists in the world, and even all that the universe holds within itself.

'But what a wonderful phenomenon', one might say, 'I never thought that the mind could be so large. I thought my mind was even smaller than my body, that it was hidden somewhere in a corner of my brain.' The understanding of mind indeed widens one's outlook on life. It first produces bewilderment; then the vision of the nature of God, which is a phenomenon in itself, becomes revealed.

Does one then see all those whom one has known while on earth? Yes, especially those whom one has loved most and hated most.

What will be the atmosphere of that world? It will be the re-echo of the same atmosphere which one has created in this world. If one has learned while on earth how to create joy and happiness for oneself and for others, in the other world that joy and happiness surrounds one. If one has sown the seed of poison while on earth, the fruits of these one must reap there. That is where one sees justice as the nature of life.★

The idea of the prophets, which one finds in the ancient Scriptures, that there will be a Judgment Day and that man will be called before the great Judge to answer for his deeds, must not be understood literally. In the first place the Judge would not have sufficient time to hear the numberless cases, since every soul would have a world full of faults: his merits would amount to nothing when compared with his faults. No, Judgment Day is every day, and man knows it as his sight becomes keener. Every hour, every moment in life has its judgment. As the Prophet said, one will have to give account for every grain of corn one eats. There is no doubt about it; but why Judgment Day has been especially mentioned in the Scriptures as taking place in the hereafter, is because in the hereafter one cover has been lifted from the soul. Therefore, the judgment which every soul experiences here on earth and yet remains ignorant of, being unconscious of it, becomes more clearly manifest to the view of the soul after it has passed from this earth.

What connection has the soul which has passed from the

★See Appendix, page 186 on God's Justice.

earth with those who are still on the earth? No doubt there is a wall now which divides those on this earth from those on the other plane, yet the connection of the heart still keeps intact and it remains unbroken as long as the link of sympathy is there. But why do the lovers of those who have passed away from the earth not know of the condition of their beloved ones on the other side? They know it in their souls, but the veils of the outer illusions of the physical world cover their hearts, therefore they cannot bring through clear reflections. Besides, it is not only the link of love and sympathy but the belief in the hereafter to the extent of conviction in that belief, which lifts those still on earth to know about their beloved ones who have passed over to the other side. Those who deny the hereafter, deny to themselves that knowledge which is the essence of all learning.

It is easier for those who have passed from the earth to the other side to get in touch with those on earth, for they have one veil less than those on earth.

Are the souls who have passed away nearer to us than those who live with us on earth?

In one way they are nearer, and in another way they are farther. They are nearer in this way that, if we wanted to get in touch with them or they with us, it is more quickly and more easily done than with the souls who are here on earth; but when we look at the difference of the plane on which they live and our plane, they are farther than those on earth. So in another way it is easier for those who live on the same plane, because here there are different means of communication.

How do the souls who have passed away move from place to place?

They move from place to place much quicker than one on earth can imagine. Their form is not so dense as the earthly form. They are more capable of moving about than a bird. Yet they have a form, and it is for this reason that every child longs to have wings, because its soul feels deprived of that freedom which it has known. Therefore, the only consolation for a poor child is to think of fairies, that there are beings who move about with wings. It is also for this reason that one often dreams of flying.

What are these souls who have passed away engaged in doing?

They are engaged in doing the same things which they were doing before. Everything they had here they have there, but with a greater freedom, because here they cannot improve upon it, hindered by the limitations of the earthly law. There they can improve, if there is only the impulse towards improvement behind them.

They do everything with the mind?

Yes.

Is the world of mind more beautiful than nature on earth?

Certainly it is, for mind is nature also. Mind is an improvement upon nature, and nature at the same time; for instance, the idea of paradise is an improvement upon nature. Now on earth paradise is mere imagination, but in the hereafter the same idea will become a reality.

Is it natural for the souls who have passed to come in contact with the souls on earth?

Yes, it is quite natural.

Do the souls in the hereafter live on old or on new impressions?

It is a continuation of the impressions, of all that the soul has collected. If he knows how to throw them off, he need not take them with him.

Then comes the question of mysticism. That is why the wise have always said: have constructive thoughts, a tendency to joy, to create beauty and happiness for ourselves and for others, so that it will multiply and become more and more abundant. Then in the hereafter it will make a world of happiness if we continue to keep that idea through life. It is the whole religion and the whole philosophy there.

CHAPTER 36

12th September, 1923, 5.30 p.m.

WHAT does a soul do after having arrived at the sphere of the *djinn* on its return journey? It continues to do the same things which it was doing while on earth, right or wrong, good or evil. It goes along the same lines that it went on through life.

Is there no progress for that soul? Yes, there is, but in the same direction; no ultimate change necessarily takes place. Yes, the soul finds itself in clearer spheres, therefore it knows its way better than it had known before when on earth.

What is its destination? The same destination, though it may be hidden under a thousand objects. Every soul is bound for the same goal. How can it be otherwise? Think how a person becomes attached to a place where he has been before, think how one is attracted to a spot in a solitude where once one has sat and enjoyed the beauty of nature. How much then must the soul be attracted, either consciously or unconsciously, to its source which is its eternal abode.

What connection do the souls which have passed from the earth have with those whom they have left on the earth? No particular connection, except the connection which is made by the link of love and sympathy.

Do they all know of the conditions on the earth? Yes, if they care to. How can they know them, if they care to? Is there no wall between the people on the earth and those who have passed away? Yes, there is a wall which only stands before those who are still on the earth, but not before the ones who have passed over to the other side. They rise above this wall, so they see, if they care to see, the conditions of the world as clearly as we do and even more so.

Do they need some medium in order to observe the conditions on earth, or can they observe without any medium? No, they must have a medium, a medium on the earth, as their instrument, for they must have the physical eyes to see, the physical ears to hear, the physical senses to experience life in the physical world.

Then what do they do in order to experience life in the

physical world? They seek an accommodation in the heart of a being on the earth; they focus themselves on the mind of that person, and receive through this medium all the knowledge and experience of this earth that they desire, as clearly as the person himself could do it. For instance, if the spirit of a scientist wishes to learn something from the earth and happens to focus himself upon the mind of an artist, the artist who knows nothing about science will, perhaps, remain as ignorant as before of science (except some vague idea of scientific discovery which will be felt by the mind of this artist) and yet, through this artist, the spirit of the scientist will learn all he wishes.

Do the spirits* always learn from the earth, or do they teach those on the earth? Both, they learn as well as they teach.

Are there any spirits who care little for the life they have left behind? Many, and among them good ones who are only concerned with the journey onwards. It is those, as a rule, whose heart is still attached to life on earth, and in whose heart interest for the journey onwards has not yet been kindled, who are inclined to keep in communication with the earth. Yet there are exceptions. There are spirits who, out of kindness to one, to a few, or to many wish still to keep a connection with the earth in order to serve and to be useful. The spirits of these latter kind still go on advancing towards the goal, instead of being detained when they communicate with the people on the earth.

What connection have the returning spirits with the *djinn*-inhabitants of the sphere of the *djinns*? They are as far removed from them as one planet is from another[62], though in the same universe. Do they ever meet with the inhabitants of that sphere? Yes, they do, but only such spirits as are not closed in, or imprisoned, or captive in their own world, those who have gained that strength and power, even while on earth, to break any ropes that bind them, and liberate themselves from all situations however difficult.

How do these brave ones arrive at this stage? By rising above themselves. If this limited self which makes the false ego is broken, and one has risen above the limitations of life on all planes of existence, the soul will break the boundaries and will

*Cf. page 50: the soul with the mind is called spirit.

experience that liberation which is the longing of every soul.

Is the progress of the soul hindered by being called back to the earth by mediums and sorrowing friends?

Certainly. Suppose a person was going from here to Paris. He has not yet gone as far as that door and someone calls him: 'Please stop, come here, I want you!' Perhaps he has gone farther and then a person calls: 'Please stop, I want to speak to you!' It means that he will always be detained, he will never be able to reach Paris; the purpose towards which he was going is hindered. It is meant now that he must go farther. To call him backward, I should think, is a fault against nature itself. With all our love and affection for the one we love, if it happens that the soul has passed and is going forward, it is better to help that soul to go forward more easily. And that one can do by sending one's loving thoughts.

People sometimes tell me: 'I have loved someone so much that I would not like him to go so far that I might not be able to reach him. Will he stay in the same place until I come?' It is most amusing, wishing to detain a person! If it were meant that they should be together, he would not have gone. Let him go! It is for his good. Detaining him would be pulling him back from that progress which is the longing of every soul.

Can souls from the other side communicate with souls on earth in order to bring them the conviction of the reality of the spirit world?

There are many souls which communicate with people on earth, but people on earth do not clearly receive their communications. Yet at the same time they receive them unconsciously, and very often they do errands, thinking that they are doing them of their free will, or because they wish to do it. Really speaking they are doing an errand for a spirit gone beyond.

In order to give to a person the conviction of the

existence of the world above, why should spirits strive? Why should man not develop his faith? If man is so obstinate as to keep away from developing himself, he will keep the same obstinacy in the other world, he will keep away from development even in the spirit world. So the angels need not come to wake him, for in man is the possibility of faith. The interference of the *djinn* world is not necessary.

Are there in the *djinn* and angelic world opportunities for souls to do the same things as they were busy with on earth? How can that be?

That can be. Nothing is impossible. Why should it not be? Why should not builders of houses go on building, cooks go on cooking? Some people will need to be cooked for, for there will be those who eat.

Do the spirits have day and night, sunrise and sunset?

Certainly they have.

Do they have farms and factories?

Certainly. All things that you have here, you have there, made exactly on the same model.

Can the souls who come to realization here go straight back to God, without stopping in the *djinn* and angelic world?

But it is the same way! They go by the same way – the way they came: that is the way to God! The ones who go to God do not stop here. Even on the earth they can go to God – not be on the earth! There is no condition of having to go to God through the outer death. No. Crucifixion is the condition which the Sufi calls *fanā'*. They can go to God even from here, for God is nearer to them than any sphere of angels, or anything else.

To the *djinn* world it is perhaps a journey of one step; to the angelic world two steps; but to God – no journey, He is there. If one was only conscious, He is there.

Now, to this question I can also say: can the last or highest stage that the soul perceives be attained without experiencing the *djinn* world? I should say: yes, but there is no joy in it. The joy of life is the joy of the journey. If one closed one's eyes and was put immediately on the top of the Himalayas, one would not enjoy it so much as the one who would climb from height to height, see the different scenery, meet with different people and breathe the different atmosphere and air. That is the joy of it. If he was put there with closed eyes, he would be frightened. The whole joy is of the journey.

Will you tell us something about the scenery of the *djinn* world? Does that world interpenetrate this world?

The scenery of the *djinn* world is peculiar to itself. It is a negative state of what one sees positive in this world, but more in beauty than what one sees on the earth.

In this way it interpenetrates, but at the same time it has its own peculiarity, which is incomparable with the beauty of this earth. The reason is that the manifestation on this plane has more limitations owing to its rigidity. The higher the world, the less are the limitations to be met with.

CHAPTER 37

14th September, 1923, 3.30 p.m.

THE soul which functions on its way to manifestation in different bodies, covering itself in this manner with one body over another, has a power which it uses to a smaller or greater degree in the renewing of the tissues of the body and in healing it. The child born into a family in which there are physical infirmities is often born already healed from hereditary conditions, and with its tissues renewed. The reason is that, because the soul is the divine breath, it purifies, revivifies and heals the instrument in which it functions.

On its return journey the soul shows the same phenomenon in a different way. Freeing itself from all the impressions of illness, of sadness, of misery which the soul has experienced while on earth and has taken into the spirit world, it heals its own being, and renews the tissues of that body which still remains with it after it has left the physical body. It purifies itself from all illness and the impression of illness, and thus renews the life in the spirit world in accordance with its grade of evolution. Apart from evolution, it is the tendency of the soul to reject all that is foreign to it, either from the physical body, or from the mental body which it still has in the spirit world.

The soul is on a continual journey. On whatever plane it is, it is journeying all the time, and on this journey it has a purpose to accomplish, many purposes contained and hidden in one purpose. There are objectives which remain unfulfilled in one's lifetime on earth. They are accomplished in the further journey in the spirit world, for nothing that the human heart has once desired remains unfulfilled. If it is not fulfilled here, it is accomplished in the hereafter. The desire of the human soul is the wish of God, small or great, right or wrong, and it has a moment of fulfilment. If that moment does not come while the soul is on the earth plane, it comes in its further journey, in the spirit world.

The soul proves its divine origin on all planes of existence wherever it happens to pass, in creating for itself all it desires, in producing for itself its heart's object, in gratifying itself with all it wishes, and in attracting and drawing to itself all that it wants. The source of the soul is perfect, and so is its goal. Therefore, even through its limitation, the soul has a spark of perfection. The nature of perfection is: no want. The limitation that the soul experiences is on the earth, where it lives the life of limitation. Still, its one desire is perfection, to achieve and obtain all it wants. So this want is supplied for the very reason that the Perfect One, even in the world of variety, does everything possible to experience perfection.

> Is there no illness or impression of illness on the *djinn* plane?
>
> Yes, there is. As there are illnesses on the plane of the earth, so there are certain discomforts on the

other plane. But in telling you of the healing power of the soul, I have explained that it heals the body in which it functions even on the earth; and the illnesses that it takes from the earth it heals again in the hereafter. No doubt the discomforts of that plane still remain, for life is a continual struggle. The struggle there is easier, for the reason that the facilities on the other plane are greater, while the limitations on this plane are great.

Can souls, by evil living and evil doing, deliberately kill their spirits and perish?

No, they only cover themselves by clouds of ignorance, which causes discomfort. But no soul is killed; the soul is not meant to perish.

Do children who die as infants come to maturity in the spiritual world?

Yes, they do. Often on the *djinn* plane, and sometimes on the plane of the angels. It depends upon the quality of the soul and upon the object they were meant to accomplish.

You said: the desire of the soul is the wish of God, small or great, right or wrong. How can the wish of God be wrong?

There are many things for which man accuses God of having done wrong! It is only out of his respect and his worshipful attitude to God that he does not say anything; but if he was made free, he would have a thousand accusations. I think there is no person in the world who can be accused so many times for wrongdoing as God! The reason is that it is our limited self which judges, which is not capable of judging.

CHAPTER 38

14th September, 1923, 5.30 p.m.

BOTH in the soul's coming to earth and in its return there is a process to be seen. When coming to earth it is adorning itself with the veils of the particular planes through which it passes, and on its return it unveils itself from the bodies it has adopted for its convenience in experiencing those particular planes. In this way there is a process of covering and uncovering. The soul, so to speak, throws off its garment on the same plane from which it borrowed it, when it has no more to do with it.

Then what becomes of these bodies? The earthly bodies are composed of physical atoms, and so all that has been composed decomposes and returns to its own element: breath to air, heat to fire, liquid to water and matter to earth. In spite of all the divers aspects in which the body may apparently be absorbed – various insects may eat it, birds may share it in their food, wild animals may devour it, or it may be swallowed by a fish, in time it may turn into the soil or it may be used to nourish a plant or a tree – in every case the first rule remains.★

As the physical body composes and decomposes, so does the mental or spirit body – a body which has an incomparably longer life than the physical body has on the earth. Its end is similar to the end of the physical body. When the soul unveils itself of its mental garb, this garb falls flat, as did the body of the earth, in that plane to which it belongs; for it is not the body which has strength to stand: the strength of standing belongs to the soul. It is therefore that man, in whom the soul manifests in the most pronounced form, stands upright, all animals bowing and bending according to their natural form.

Is the decomposing of the spirit body used in making the bodies there? Certainly it is. Not in such a crude way as happens with the earthly body, but in a much finer way, for this is a finer body. There is joy in the composing and decomposing of this body, as there is even some pleasure in the composing and decomposing of the physical body.

★i.e. everything returns to its own element.

THE SOUL TOWARDS THE GOAL

What does the body that the soul wears on the spirit plane look like? It looks exactly the same as one was on the earth. Why must it be so? Because of man's love for his body. Does it change? Yes, if he wishes it to change. If the soul wishes it to be changed, it can be changed according to its own ideal. It can be made as young and as beautiful as possible, but it must be remembered that by nature the soul becomes so attached to its form that it clings to it, and as a rule it does not like to become different.

The condition of the next world is most like the condition of the dream world. In dreams one does not see oneself very different from what one appears to be (except in some cases and at some times, and for that there are reasons). Nevertheless the power that the soul has in the next world is much greater than that which it has in this world of limitations. The soul in the other world, so to speak, matures and finds within itself the power of which it was ignorant through its life on earth, the power of creating and producing all that it wishes. Its movements not being so much hindered by time and space, it is capable of accomplishing and of doing for itself things which are difficult for the same soul to do and accomplish on the earth plane.

> Do souls on the spiritual plane retain the memory and knowledge of their experience on the earth?
>
> Retain? They are engraved with it. It is just like a dyed cloth which has its colours and impressions printed upon it. It is imprinted with it. With this the soul has made its world. The soul comes alone, but goes taking a world with it. And really speaking, the soul would have liked to take the earthly body if it could, but it is not allowed there. Therefore, it has to leave it here.
>
> What do you mean by 'pleasure in decomposing the physical body'?
>
> I can only tell you this by giving the example of a drunken man. He knows that the alcohol he drinks is poison. It is killing the germs of his body and blood, and doing him all harm. Yet that very reason of decomposing gives him joy. The dying process

gives him joy; gradual dying is his pleasure. When I once asked a drunken man: 'Oh why are you doing this drinking all the time, killing yourself!', he answered: 'I don't care, I would rather die than not drink.' Because it is the pleasure of dying; there is a pleasure in dying.

Is there an advantage for the animal when it is used as food for man?

It is not an advantage for the individual animal, but it is an advantage for the whole. All that is absorbed by man, either in the way of eating, or as a flower, it is all blessed, because in man the soul has reached its ultimate state. Therefore, to give to that soul an experience or a pleasure, or life, or strength, or satisfaction – whatever it is used for – it is all used for its best purpose, for it is used for the best expression of the soul.

Of course, when a person stands on another level, he can see it from another point of view. From that point of view he may see the justice or injustice of it. But the first point of view has its reason too.

CHAPTER 39

15th September, 1923, 3.30 p.m.

A soul which has passed from the earth and is in the spirit world can still live on the earth in one way, and that way is the transmigration of the soul.[63] Very often people have wrongly explained this idea, when they have said that the spirit takes hold of a dead body and, entering it, makes use of it. The body once dead is dead, it has entered upon the process of returning to its own origin. It has lost that magnetism which attracts the soul and holds it in order to allow it to function in the physical body. If the dead body had the magnetism, then it would not have allowed the soul to return, it would have held it back; for it is the body which holds the soul to the earth: the soul has a pull from within which draws it continually towards its source.

But there are many living dead, in the good sense[64] or in the bad sense of the word. It is in these cases that a single-pointed spirit takes hold of their minds and bodies as its own instruments, using them to its best advantage. It is this which is generally known as obsession. In point of fact, there is no soul who has not experienced obsession in the true sense of the word, for there are moments in one's everyday life when those on the other side take the souls on the earth as their medium through which to experience life on the earth.

Transmigration of the soul is a much deeper impression upon the soul than that which obsession gives; for in time the spirit which enters into the being of a person on earth, makes that person entirely void of himself. He loses in time his identity and becomes like the spirit which has obsessed him, not only in his thought, speech and action, but also in his attitude and outlook; in his habits and manners, even in his looks he becomes the entity which obsesses him.

Might one say, 'Then it is a good thing from a mystical point of view to become thus selfless?' No, this is not the way of being selfless, in this way one is robbed of the self. The mystical way of being selfless is to realize the self by unveiling the self from its numberless covers which make the false ego.

> Why does the spiritualist go into a trance before getting his message from the spirits?

> He must die in order to reach the dead. That is the condition.

> Should a person, in a normal state of mind or in trance, give in to an obsession to automatic writing, or should he resist this tendency?

> Every soul must not take upon itself such a risk of attempting anything in the line of phenomena, because it is full of danger for a soul unacquainted with such things. If they ever want to have any experience in that way, they must first of all find a teacher in whom they have full trust, and then ask him if they are fit for it.

CHAPTER 40

15th September, 1923, 5.30 p.m.

THE soul on its return towards the goal, while in the sphere of the *djinns* has some riches which it collected during its life on earth in the form of merits, qualities, experiences, convictions, talents, attitude and a certain outlook on life, although on its passing it has returned the belongings of the earth to the earth. These riches the soul in the spirit world offers, allows them to be taken from it, and imparts them to the souls coming from their source who are on their way to the earth. The souls on their way to the earth, full of heavenly bliss but poor in earthly riches, purchase the current coin of the earth in the *djinn* plane. Guarantees, contracts, mortgages and all the accounts that the spirit had left unfinished on the earth – these they undertake to pay or to receive when coming on the earth.

Among these souls which come to the earth there are some which take from one spirit all they can as their heritage from the spirit world, and some take from many. The souls who absorb, attract, conceive and receive all that is given to them on the spirit plane have, perhaps, received more from one spirit than all the other gifts they have received from various other spirits they have met. Does this exchange rob the spirit on its way to the goal of its merits and qualities? No, not in the least. The riches that the soul can take to the sphere of the *djinn* are safe and secure. Any knowledge or learning, merit or talent given to another person is not lost by the person who gives. It only makes the giver richer still.

When the Hindus said in ancient times to a wicked person: 'Next time you are born you will come back as a dog or a monkey', it was to tell him, who did not know the end of life, except about himself, that his animal qualities would be brought back again as the heritage of the animal world, so that he would not come again to the knowledge of his human friends as a man, but as an animal. When they said: 'Your good actions will bring you back as a better person, as a higher person', it was said in the sense that the man, who did not know the two extreme poles of his soul, might understand that no good action would be lost. For the man who had no hope in the hereafter, as he did not know what it was, and who only knew of life as lived on the earth, it was a consolation to know that all the good he had done would come again. And it was true in that sense of the theory which was thus explained.

The soul which comes from above has no name or form, has no particular identity. It makes no difference to that soul what it is called. Since it has no name it might just as well adopt the name of the coat which was put on it, as that is the nature of life. The robe of justice put upon a person makes him a judge, and the uniform of a policeman makes him a constable. The judge was not born a judge, nor the constable a policeman. They were born on earth nameless, if not formless. Distinctions and differences belong to the lower world, not to the higher. Therefore the Sufi does not argue against the idea of reincarnation. The difference is only in words. It is necessary that a precaution be taken that the door may be kept open for souls who wish to enter the kingdom of God, that they may not feel bound by a dogma that they will have to be dragged back by their *karmā* after they have left the earth plane.★

The soul of man is the spark of God. Though God is helpless on the earth, still He is all powerful in heaven, and by teaching the prayer: 'Thy kingdom come, Thy will be done on earth as it is in heaven', the Master has given a key to every soul who repeats this prayer, a key to open that door wherein is the secret of that almighty power and perfect wisdom, which raises the soul above all limitations.

> What did you mean by saying that God is helpless on earth, but all powerful in heaven?

> For the very reason that in the world God is divided into different personalities, and in heaven God remains in one Personality; then all His power is in one, therefore His power is unlimited. But His object in all the limited personalities which are on the earth is the same as His object in heaven: that His will be done. Therefore every person, whether poor or rich, has the wish: my will be done. Whose desire

★See Appendix, page 191 on Reincarnation.

is it? God's desire. But this desire can be fulfilled only if man will give up his desire to the desire of God. For this desire can only be fulfilled on one condition, and that condition is: if he can give himself up for the Self of God. That is the meaning of crucifixion: to crucify the lower self, to give up the false self, for the Self of God. Then there is perfection, then His will is done. That soul is His will. Once he has given up his own will, then he is the will of God.

Can a soul on its downward journey receive bad qualities as well as good qualities from returning souls?

Certainly, both. How can there be light without shade? It is the light and shade which make the picture complete.

They have a certain choice?

Yes. Every step they go and every impression they receive becomes their guide to their further step. For instance, we are walking in a forest; we do not know the way, we only walk by the inspiration we receive from all we see. So we go. In the same way the impression on the soul comes from the place where it starts, and hearing that music it always goes where that music is; all the vibrations and all the beauty to which it becomes accustomed, the soul goes towards it and receives it. Everyone is attracted to that beauty which particularly appeals to his mind, and that mind has a preparation beforehand which makes it appreciate that particular beauty.

It begins first with music. That music is the note of the soul. The next step is that the beauty appears outwardly, and in this way it goes on.

I have spoken of these three stages, the *djinn*, human and angelic plane, for the facility of my *murīds*, to enable them to understand; just like the musicians who have given seven notes for the facility of those who want to study music. But are there seven notes? No, there are as many notes as one can create or perceive.

For instance, the musicians in India have four quarter tones between two notes. A musician playing the vina may realize that there are four quarter tones; but is it finished with four? No, there could be a thousand tones, according to the power of our senses. The limited range of our hearing causes us not to perceive music finer than that; only the grades of distinction are perceptible to our ears.

So the different planes are perceptible, but there is one life running through them – there is no gap between them – there are walls to divide them. What are these walls? They are, like bars in music, for our perception, because we are unable to go beyond. Dividing is for our understanding.

In reality life is – from God to the earth and from the earth to God – one single stream of life running through without a gap. What do we call this space? We may call it empty, but is it empty? Our eyes are so limited that we can only see a certain thickness of substance. If it is not so thick we cannot see it, we call it 'nothing', we say, 'It is nothing'. But it is something out of which all things come.

CHAPTER 41

17th September, 1923, 3.30 p.m.

DOES the spirit impart its merits, talents, experience and knowledge consciously or unconsciously to the new coming soul passing through the spirit spheres towards the earth? Sometimes it imparts consciously, in some cases unconsciously. But in the conscious action there is the greatest pleasure for the spirit. For this soul, which is taking the knowledge from a spirit as its heritage from the sphere of the *djinn*, is considered by the spirit as a child is by his parents, or a pupil by his teacher. In giving the heritage to this soul there is great joy for that spirit.

Do they keep connection in any way? No connection except a sympathetic link, for one goes to the North, while the other goes to the South; one ascending to heaven, the other descending to the earth. A connection or an attachment between them would do nothing but hinder the progress of both.

A soul lives in the spirit world while it is busy accomplishing the purpose of its life, which may last for thousands of years. Does a soul in the spirit world continue to do the same work which it did during its life on the earth? Yes, it does in the beginning, but it is not bound to the same work, for the reason that it is not subject to the same limitations as it was while on earth. The soul eventually rises to that standard which was the standard of its ideal; it does that work which was its desire.

Are there difficulties in the spirit world, as on the earth, in doing something and in accomplishing something? Certainly there are, but not as many as here on the earth.

But what if there were one object that was desired by various spirits? How can they all attain to it? Will they all get some particles of that object? And if it be a living being, what then? The law of that world is different from the law of this world of limitations. There, souls will find in abundance all which is scarcely to be found here on earth.

The picture of the spirit world is given in the story of Krishna. The Gopis of Vrindavan[65] all requested the young Krishna to dance with them. Krishna smiled and answered each one: 'On the night of the full moon.' All the Gopis gathered in the valley of Vrindavan and a miracle happened. However many Gopis there were, there were as many Krishnas, and every Gopi had a dance with Krishna; all had their desire fulfilled. This is a symbolical way of teaching that the one divine Being may be found by every soul.

The spirit world is incomprehensible to the mind which is only acquainted with the laws of the physical world. An individual who is a limited being here, is as a world there. A soul is a person here and a planet there. When one considers the helplessness of this plane, one cannot for a single moment imagine the greatness, the facility, the convenience, the comfort and the possibilities of the next world. It is human nature that all which is unknown to man – with all its greatness and riches – means nothing to him.

A pessimist came to 'Alī[66] and said: 'Is there really a hereafter for which you are preparing by telling us to refrain from things of our desire and to live a life of goodness and piety? What if there is no such thing as a hereafter?' Ali answered: 'If there is no such thing as a hereafter, I shall be in the same boat as you are, and if there be a hereafter, then I shall be the gainer and you will be the loser.'

Life lives and death dies. The one who lives will live, must live. There is no alternative.

> Has it ever happened that a soul which had meant to go forward to the physical plane remained in the sphere of the *djinn* for the love of a soul there?

> It does happen very often. It is love that takes one forward in one's progress, and again sometimes it is love which deters one from progressing. There is a difference between higher and lower love. It is higher love which takes one forward, and it is lower love that holds one back. When love is not high enough it has not the power to go forward, and sometimes it pins one against the same point where one stands. Love is the battery which should be used to go forward.

> Could a soul also persuade another soul which was meant to stay in the *djinn* plane to go with it to the earth?

> No, once a soul has individualized itself in a certain plane, it becomes the inhabitant of that plane; it does not go forward, it stops as long as it wishes to stop, or as it is meant to stop, which means equal to thousands of years of this earthly plane. It can go quicker, it is possible – like a person who wishes to finish his life here on the earthly plane. So it is possible there also.

> How do the souls coming out get impressions from the souls coming back from the earth?

> They absorb, conceive, learn and receive all that is given to them by the souls coming from the earth.

What mostly happens is by reflection: reflection of the souls coming from the earth falling upon the souls coming from heaven. They become impressed just like an impression upon a photographic plate: as they come on earth, the photographic plate is developed, and when on earth the photo is finished.

Does it take a long time to get the impressions? Is the impression imparted instantaneously, or is it like taking lessons?

As a rule the reflection is just like a photographic plate. The difference is of the quality of the soul. There is one soul upon which the impression is made instantly, there is another soul which needs time to take the impression. It is because of the intensity of the power and the radiance that the soul brings with itself. It is like children born on earth: some are intelligent, quick to perceive and willing to learn, others are unwilling to learn and not quick in perception.

Do several souls, impressed by the same spirit, resemble each other, and do they recognize each other when on earth?

They do resemble each other as the children of the same parents, and yet they are different as brothers and sisters differ from one another. They are attracted to one another and they find their thoughts and ideas akin to each other. Also they show this nearness in the similarity of their works.

As what do the souls who are spiritually evolved live in the hereafter?

As planets. There are numberless planets. The difference will be between large planets and small planets, according to their outlook: whether they are large souls or small souls. As large as they will be here, so large a planet they will be there.

In the Old Testament one reads that the earth was made first and the heaven afterwards. This means that it is the souls as planets which will form the cosmos there in the spiritual world. Therefore the heaven, or the cosmos was dependent on the creation of this earth to make the cosmos perfect there.

Do the planets of different souls interpenetrate, or are they entirely apart from one another?

They are entirely apart one from the other; at the same time the law of the cosmic system is the same here and in the next world, for they all hold one another by their power of magnetism and by their power of attraction. So we human beings on earth attract one another and repel one another, subject to the law of magnetism. Furthermore, as human beings on the earth we each stand apart, and yet have influence on one another, have friendship, attachment and acquaintance, a connection, a relation; the same can be found in the cosmic system with the planets; and the same law is to be seen in the sphere of the *djinns*.

Does the planet of each soul contain just the things the soul thinks or imagines, or other things also?

Just the things the soul thinks or imagines – also things which that soul creates.

CHAPTER 42

17th September, 1923, 5.30 p.m.

LIFE in the sphere of the *djinns* is the phenomenon of mind. The mind is not the same there. With all the thoughts and imaginations which it carries from the earth to that plane the mind, which is a mind here on earth, is the whole being there on the return journey. Thoughts are imaginations here, but reality there. One thinks here, but the same action there, instead of a thought, becomes a deed; for action, which here depends upon the physical body, is there the act of mind.

There is a picture of this idea in a story[50]. A man who had heard of the existence of a tree of desire was once travelling. He happened to come under the shade of a tree, which was restful and cooling, so he sat there leaning against it. He said to himself: 'How beautiful is nature, how cooling is the shade of this tree, and the breeze is most exhilarating. If only I had a soft carpet to sit on and some cushions to lean against.' No sooner had he thought about it than he saw himself sitting in the midst of soft cushions. 'How wonderful', he thought, 'to have got this.' But now he thought: 'If only I had a glass of cooling drink.' Thereupon a fairy appeared with a glass of cold drink, most delicious. He enjoyed it, but said: 'I would like a dinner, a good dinner.' No sooner had he thought of a dinner than a gold tray was brought to him, beautifully arranged dishes of all sorts. Now he thought: 'If only I had a chariot, that I might take a drive into the forest.' And a four-horse chariot was already there, the coachmen greeting him with bent heads. He thought: 'Everything I desire comes without any effort. I wonder if it is true, or all a dream.' No sooner had he thought this, than everything disappeared, and he found himself sitting on the same ground leaning against the tree.

This is the picture of the spirit world. It is the world of the optimist, the pessimist has no share in its great glory, for the reason that he refuses to accept the possibility which is the nature of life. Thereby he denies to himself all he desires, and the possibility of achieving his desires. The pessimist stands against his own light and mars his own object, here and even more so in the hereafter, where desire is the seed which is sown in the soil of the spirit world, while optimism is the water which rears the plant, and the Intelligence at the same time gives that sunshine which helps the plant to flourish, on the earth as well as in the spheres of the *djinns*.

Is there death for the spirits in the sphere of the *djinns*? Yes, but after a much longer time, a death that is not so severe as on the earthly plane, where everything is crude and coarse; but a change is slightly felt after a very long time of the fulfilment of every desire. What causes this death? Are there illnesses or diseases? Yes, there are discomforts and pains peculiar to that sphere, not to be compared with the diseases on the plane of the earth. What especially brings about death in the sphere of the *djinn* is the moment when hope gives way, and there is no ambition left. It is the loss of enthusiasm which is death there, and the cause of death here on the earth.

THE SOUL TOWARDS THE GOAL

Souls in the spirit world have more control over their life and death than those on the earth. The world of the spirit is its own world. It is a planet. When it loses that strength and magnetism which holds the soul functioning in it, it falls like a star from heaven, and the soul departs to its own origin.

As the spirit world brings the fulfilment of every desire, does the soul who has died before death and has therefore no desires, stay there only a short time?

'Died before death', what do you mean by that? That soul is the king of the spirit world! and never think that the one who has died before death has no desire. The desire springs up again, only he is not beneath the desire, he is above the desire. The picture of the God Vishnu[10] shows this: Vishnu sitting upon the lotus. Lotus is the desire, every petal of the lotus is a desire. Sitting upon the lotus does not mean that he does not possess desire, but shows that the desire is under him, instead of over his head; it shows that he is the master of desire.

Are the desires which we call passions also fulfilled in the *djinn* world? Or are passions more bound to the earth?

Every desire. When the tree of passion is raised, it reaches as far as the world of the *djinn*, only not in the same sense as it is on earth.

Are there courtship and marriage and are there children born on the spirit plane?

It is not necessary that the law of the spiritual plane should work so much in accordance with the law of the physical plane. Even on the physical plane the law differs. Among the living creatures there are some who are egg-born, and there are different ones. Then there are living creatures who are born out of the animal world, and others who come from the leaves and fruits. It is quite a different process. When there are such varieties here, the laws of the spirit world must not be compared exactly with the

165

laws of this world. Still, one law remains all through in all planes, and that is the law of duality, negative and positive, the law of expression and conception. Every issue, in whatever plane it comes, is subject to this law.

Shall we see our goal in the *djinn* sphere while here it is in the dark?

Yes, for the possibilities of the sphere of the *djinn* are greater than here on earth, owing to the limitations caused by earthly life.

Is the length of time that the spirit remains in the plane of the *djinns* dependent upon the life on earth?

Not necessarily, but to some extent there is a relationship between life in the spirit world and life on earth. For what one takes from life on earth is according to the largeness of one's life, and gives the task one has to perform there. If a person has stayed on the earth a shorter time, his task is smaller, so the duration of his stay in the world of *djinns* will be less.

However, there is another condition. The one who has stayed less here, has much more to accomplish there, than the one who has stayed longer here on the earth. This is to be taken more in a spiritual sense, for the one who has attained spirituality here, it is not a necessity that he should stay here longer, unless it is his desire. But in the case of the others, it is necessary for them to stay there longer to accomplish their task.

Do spirits meet with accidents or get killed?

They meet with all sorts of experiences in the spirit world as on earth.

When a spirit dies, do those who are around him sorrow over his death?

Certainly they do. Not so much perhaps as on earth.

Are there in the spirit plane different languages, races, nations?

There are as many races, nationalities and languages

as on earth. There are wars, battles and peace.

Will there be no silence in the world of *djinns*?

Yes, silence is a necessity, just as sleep. Where there is an activity there is repose. Silence is the reaction to work and that must be there. But there will be action also.

CHAPTER 43

Autumn, 1923

[67]WHAT will be the mystery hidden behind the accomplishment of all desire in the world next to the earth plane? Will-power with optimism. It is conviction which is called *yaqīn* by the Sufis; that will be the guiding light which will illuminate the path of the soul in the spiritual world. What will hinder the progress of the spirits is the lack of the same, though it is not necessarily the case that the soul who has been pessimistic here must remain pessimistic in the next world. It is possible that its journey onward will bring about a change once the soul becomes acquainted with the mysteries of hopefulness.

In what way will spirits communicate with one another? All spirits will not necessarily communicate. Only those spirits who wish to communicate will do so. In what language? In their own language. If spirits did not know one another's language in the spirit world, there would not be such difficulty as on earth, for there is one common language on that plane, a language which is the language of the spirit.

[Question not recorded]

We shall know each other better there than here, because that is the plane where the knowledge is possible, which is not possible here. Do we not say to our friends here, 'I cannot understand you. You are a mystery to me'? Perhaps you have been with a friend for fifty years, and yet he is still a mystery. That mystery becomes known, that knot is unravelled, as one goes farther.

For instance, the language of the spheres of the

djinns is more indistinct compared with the language of the earth, and yet more expressive. The language of the sphere of the angels is still less distinct, and even more expressive than that of the *djinns*.

It is this mystery which can be found in the miracle of the descending of the Holy Ghost, the descending of the tongues of fire upon the apostles. It is not in the outer sense of the explanation that they knew the languages of all the people in the world. They knew the language of the soul, when they touched the heavenly world, and that language of the soul expresses more than the language of the people on the earth.

CHAPTER 44

18th September, 1923, 3.30 p.m.

THE soul now enters the angelic heavens, and it is allowed to enter under the same condition as before: it has to leave all that belongs to the sphere of the *djinn* in that sphere. Thus, by uncovering itself from the garb of the spirit world, it finds its entrance into the world of the angels.

Does it take anything to the world of the angels? Yes, not thoughts, but feelings that it has collected. The life of the soul therefore in this sphere is more felt by its vibrations. Every soul that enters the heaven of the angels vibrates with the same vibrations that it has gathered during its life in the physical world and in the world of the *djinn*. The example of this is manifest to our view here, if we observe life more keenly. Every person, before he does anything or says one word, begins to vibrate aloud what he is, what he has done, what he will do.[68] There is an English saying: what you are speaks louder than what you say.

The soul, apart from the body and mind, is a sound, a note, a tone, which is called in Sanskrit *sura*. If this note is inharmonious and has dissonant vibrations, it is called in the Sanskrit language *asura*, out of tune. The soul, therefore, in the heaven of the angels has not got sins or virtues to show, nor has it a heaven or hell to experience. It does not show any particular ambition or desire; it is either in tune or out of tune. If it is in tune, it takes its place in the music of the heavens as a note in the tune. If it is not in tune, it falls short of this, producing a dissonant effect for itself and for others.

What occupation has the soul there? Its occupation is to be around the Light and Life, like the bee around the flower. What is its sustenance? Its sustenance is divine Light and divine Life. Divine beauty it sees, divine air it breathes, in the sphere of freedom it dwells, and the presence of God it enjoys. Life in the heaven of the angels is one single music, one continual music. Therefore it is that the wise of all ages have called music celestial, a divine art. The reason is that the heaven of the angels is all music. In the activity, the repose and the atmosphere there is all one harmony continually working towards greater and greater harmony.

What connection has the soul now with the spheres of the *djinn*, once it has arrived in the angelic heavens. No connection necessarily, except a sympathetic link, if it happens to have such with anyone there, or if it happens that the body in which it had functioned has given way before it has accomplished what it wanted to accomplish.

The happiness of the angelic heavens is so great that the joy of the sphere of the *djinns* cannot be compared with it, and the pleasures of the earth cannot even be talked about. For earthly pleasures are mere shadows of that happiness which belongs to the heaven of the angels, and the joy of the sphere of the *djinns* is like wine that has touched the lips but that one has never drunk. That wine one drinks on arriving at the heavens of the angels. In Sufi terminology that wine is called *kawthar*.[69]

There is a Hindu saying that there are four things which intoxicate the soul: physical energy, wealth, power and learning; but the intoxication that music gives excels all other forms of intoxication.[70] Then imagine the music of the heavens where harmony is in its fullness! What happiness that can give, man here on earth cannot imagine. If the experience of that music is known to anyone, it is to the awakened souls whose bodies are here, whose hearts are in the spheres of the *djinns*, whose souls are in the heavens of the angels and who, while on earth, can experience all the planes of existence. They term the music of the angelic spheres *sawt e sarmad*[71]; they find in it a happiness which carries them to the highest heavens, lifting them from the worries and anxieties and from all the limitations of the plane of this earth.

> How does a soul that is not in tune manage to enter the angelic heavens? Surely it must spoil the harmony for the others?

Yes, that shows that there is no peace, even in heaven. The inharmonious people follow the harmonious even as far as in heaven. But as the soul goes farther it improves, it becomes more and more in tune. At the same time the vibrations of every soul are different, one is more harmonious than the other, but they all fit in to the one music of heaven, for the reason that in music you do not want all notes alike; all different notes are necessary.

Is discord sometimes necessary for harmony?

Not at all. Discord is not necessary for harmony. It can be harmonized when there are more chords and there is a large part of harmony. Then even the dissonant notes can be taken in and they are tuned also, because the note which is in discord will come to its perfection.

There is a chance of harmony at every step even as far as in the heavens, for life is progressive, and therefore there is always hope of improvement.

The soul is continually on a journey towards improvement. Therefore even in the angelic world the soul is not yet perfect. It is going towards the goal; the perfection is in the goal, not in the soul.

Is there any difference in the degree of experiencing happiness between the soul going to manifestation and the returning soul?

Certainly there is, but this degree is like the difference of notes in music. Particularly the souls returning to the goal have acquired something from the earth and something from the sphere of the *djinn* which has influenced the tone and the rhythm of their being. Therefore they, so to speak, tell the legend of their past in the music they make in the heavens of the angels.

CHAPTER 45

18th September, 1923, 5.30 p.m.

WHAT body has the soul in the heaven of the angels? The soul – though it continues in the sphere of the *djinn* with a body of the likeness of the one it had while on earth – has undergone an enormous change, which has taken place in its body and form while in the sphere of the *djinn*. By the time it departs from there, there is hardly any trace left of the body it had in the sphere of the *djinn* and before; and when the soul reaches the angelic heavens there is still a greater change, for there it is turned into a luminous being. Its body is then of radiance, it is Light itself. The only difference is that light, as we understand it on the physical plane, is of a different character. For it is here visible, but there it is both Light and Life in one. So the Light is audible as well as visible, besides being intelligent.

One may say: but the physical body is intelligent also. Yes, it is. It is its Intelligence which we call sensitiveness. But the body in the sphere of the *djinn* is even more intelligent, and the body that remains in the angelic heavens is more intelligent still, it may be called Intelligence itself.[72]

The sizes of the bodies in the sphere of the *djinn* and in the heaven of the angels are as numerous as on the earth plane. The size of the body that the soul brings from the sphere of the *djinn* is much larger than the size of the physical body, and the size of the body brought by the soul from the angelic heavens is larger still. When the soul dons the body from the sphere of the *djinn*, that body not only covers the physical body, but also enters into it. So the body brought from the angelic heavens covers the body of the sphere of the *djinn* as well as the body of the physical plane, and yet enters into the innermost part of man's being. In this way the angelic and the *djinn* bodies not only surround the physical body, but exist within it.[73]

When the soul is on its way to the physical plane, its bodies grow, develop and become more distinct, and as the soul advances towards the goal, so its bodies become more ethereal, luminous, but indistinct.

The life of the souls in the angelic heavens is incomparably

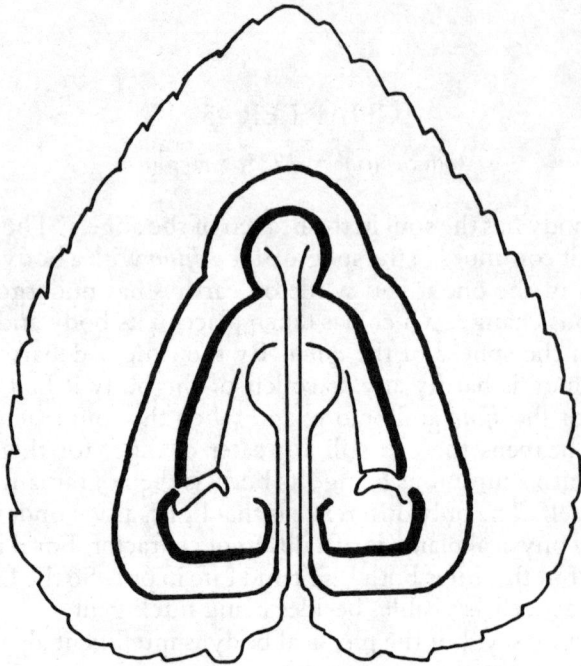

This drawing is the explanation of what we call the within. A person is apt to think of the soul as something within, smaller than the body, whereas the outermost line in this diagram is the soul. The next line is the mind, and the inner line with the hard, concrete edge is the body.

The mind stands outside the body and goes into the body at the opening which is the heart-centre. The soul which stands outside mind and body becomes also the innermost, entering the body at the centre between the eyes, the soul-centre.

Thus the soul is covered by the mind and the mind is covered by the body; at the same time the mind is covering the body and the soul is covering the mind.

longer than the life of those in the sphere of the *djinns*. No more desires, no more ambitions, no more strivings have they, only aspiration to reach further, to experience greater happiness; the tendency is to go farther and to get closer to that Light which is now within their sight. They fly around this Light like the moth around the lantern. The magic lantern which is the seeking of all souls is now within their horizon. Nothing has a greater attraction for them than this Light which is continually burning before them. They live and move and have their being in this divine Light.

Have they anything to offer to the souls going towards manifestation? Yes, their feelings. In what way do they offer them? Souls coming from the source and going towards the earth are tuned by them, are set to a certain rhythm. It is this offering which determines the line they tread in the future. The Sufis call that day of tuning *rōz-e-azal*, the day when the plan was first designed of the life of that particular soul.

Does one soul only impress the soul newly coming towards earth with its tune and rhythm, with its feeling and sentiment? No, not necessarily one soul. Many souls may impress, but it is the one impression which is dominant. Is there any link or connection established between the souls who give and take thus one from the other? Yes, a link of sympathy, a feeling of love and friendliness, an impression of joy which a soul carries with it even to the destination to which it comes on the earth. The crying of an infant is very often the expression of its longing for the angelic heavens; the smiles of an infant are a narrative of its memories of heaven and of the spheres above.

Does the returning soul which meets with the new-coming soul receive anything? It does not require much, 'it is full of joy in its approach to the culmination of life, the goal of its journey. Yet the purity that the new coming soul brings with a new Life and Light, gives ease to the soul striving towards the goal and illuminates its path.

There is almost too much that a soul has to do on the earth. There is also much that the soul has to accomplish in the spirit world, or plane of the *djinns*; but there is much less to accomplish in the heavens of the angels. For as the soul proceeds forward, so its burden becomes lightened. The only condition of proceeding forward and drawing closer to the goal is that of throwing away the heavy burden which the soul has taken upon itself throughout its journey.

If one may say that the soul lives in the spheres of the *djinns* for thousands of years, for the sake of convenience one may use the expression millions of years in speaking of the length of time that the soul passes in the heavens of the angels. At last there comes the moment when the soul is most willing to depart even from that plane of love, harmony and beauty, in order to embrace the source and goal of love, harmony and beauty which has attracted it through all the planes. As the soul approaches nearer, so it is drawn closer. It is the throwing off of that radiant garment, which is the body of the soul in the angelic heavens, that brings it to its real destination, the goal which it has continually sought, either consciously or unconsciously.

Verily, from God every soul comes, and to God is its return.

> Will you explain what the sentence means: 'The soul has sought the goal consciously or unconsciously'?

> As it approaches closer, the more conscious it becomes, because now it is within its horizon.

> Is the higher body of the soul formed from the lower body of the same soul?

> Yes, on the design of it, because it is the continuation. For instance, after coming from the earth the soul continues the same life, there is no definite break. Therefore there is something of the earth which can be taken. All cannot be taken, or the souls would not only have taken their bodies but their houses too!

> In the account of his mystical journey to the angelic heaven Dante tells how he enters the sphere of the moon and calls it 'a sphere of solid light'. Is that an imagination?

> No, it is in support of the lesson which has been given to-day, that the angels are of luminous body, as solid – that is as concrete – as the light one sees. It is Dante's own vision of this plane. The sphere of the moon is the sphere of harmony, because the moon responds to the sun. It is the respondent

attitude of the moon which is harmonious. Therefore it is the sphere of harmony, which is heaven.

From where does the soul come which appears in the angelic heaven and goes to manifestation? Where does the returning soul go, after leaving the angelic heaven?

From the Spirit of God it comes, and to the Light of God it goes.

CONCLUSION

19th September, 1923, 5.30 p.m.

WHAT is this journey taken by the soul from the source to manifestation, and from manifestation again to the same source which is its goal? Is it a journey or is it not a journey? It is not a journey objectively,[74] it is a change of experiences which makes it a story. And yet the whole story produced in moving pictures is in one film which does not travel for miles and miles, as is seen on the screen.

Do many make the journey or one?   Many while still in illusion, and one when the spirit has disillusioned itself.

Who journeys? Is it man or God?   Both, and yet one: the two ends of one line.

What is the nature and character of this manifestation?   It is an interesting dream.

What is this illusion caused by?   By cover upon cover. So the soul is covered by a thousand veils.

Do these covers give happiness to the soul?   Not happiness, but intoxication. The farther the soul is removed from its source, the greater the intoxication.

Does this intoxication suffice for the purpose of the soul and its journey?   It does in a way, but the purpose of the soul is in its longing.

And what is that longing?   Sobriety.

And how is that sobriety attained?   By throwing away the covers which have covered the soul and thus divided it from its real source and goal.

What uncovers the soul from these veils of illusion? The change which is called death. This change is either forced upon the soul against its desire, and is then called death – which is a most disagreeable experience, like snatching away the bottle of wine from a drunken man, which is at the time most painful to him – or the change is brought about at will, and the soul throws away the cover that surrounds it and attains the same experience of sobriety while on earth, even if it be but a

177

glimpse of it; the same experience at which, after millions and millions of years, the soul drunken by illusion arrives, and yet not exactly the same. The experience of the former★ is *fanā*, annihilation, but the realization of the latter★★ is *baqā*, resurrection.[75]

The soul, drawn by the magnetic power of the divine Spirit, falls into it with a joy inexpressible in words, as a loving heart lays itself down in the arms of its beloved. The increasing of this joy is so great that nothing the soul has ever experienced in its life has made it so unconscious of the self as this joy does. But this unconsciousness of the self becomes in reality the true Self – consciousness. It is then that the soul realizes fully 'I exist'. But the soul which arrives at this stage of realization consciously has a different experience. The difference is like that between a person having been pulled back with his back turned to the source, and another person having journeyed towards the goal enjoying at every step each experience he has met with, and rejoicing at every moment of this journey in approaching nearer to the goal.

What does the soul, conscious of its progress towards the goal, realize? It realizes at every veil it has thrown off a better life, a greater power, an increased inspiration, until – having passed through the spheres of the *djinns* and the heavens of the angels – it arrives at a stage when it realizes that error which it had known and yet not fully known, the error it made in identifying itself with its reflection, with its shadow, falling on these different planes; as if the sun, forgetting at that moment that the sunflower was only its footprint, had thought on looking at it, 'I am the sunflower.'

Neither on the earth plane was man his own Self, nor in the sphere of the *djinns*, nor in the heavens of the angels. He was only a captive by his own illusion – caught in a frame. Yet, he was not inside it – it was only his reflection. But he saw himself nowhere, so he could only identify himself with his various reflections, until the moment that the soul realized, 'It is I who was, if there were any. What I had thought myself to be was not myself, but was my experience. I am all that there is, and it is myself who will be, whoever there will be. It is I who am the

★ the former is the soul upon which the change is forced.
★★ the latter is the soul which brings the change about at will.

source, the traveller and the goal of this whole existence.'[76]

Verily, truth is all the religion there is, and it is truth that will save.

APPENDIX

ON THE QUESTION IF THE UNIVERSE IS GOING ON AUTOMATICALLY

(Continuation of page 46,)
18th August, 1923, 3.30 p.m.

How is the periodic coming and going of events such as cataclysms, wars etc. to be explained, as well as the possibility of purely mathematical reading of the whole life in astrology? These things seem to speak in favour of the idea that all life is an automatically running clock and that there is no liberty of action and thought. For instance, the death of a babe or a child: what is the sense of a human being dying before it has reached a certain development? It seems a great waste of energy and a great suffering in vain.

The answer to the first question, in which is asked if the whole universe is going on automatically and if there is no freewill, is: Yes, man is born in a universe that is going on automatically and he is born helpless. It is true that the condition is such. But with what is the child born? He is born with a desire to do as he wills. This desire is the proof that there is freewill, a freewill which is put to the test under all the opposing conditions and influences which the soul meets through life. To rise above all the opposing influences and to give the fullest expression to the freewill brings about that result of life, which is the fulfilment of the soul's coming on earth.

As to the second question: the reason for many things having sprung out of this automatically working universe, such as the birth of a babe who has passed soon after, in this case we must understand that, although outwardly it is automatically working, inwardly there is God. There is no mechanism without an engineer; only the Engineer does not seem to be standing by the side of the mechanism, and he is not claiming that he is the Engineer. One thinks that there is a machine going on and that there is no Engineer. If one knew that there is an Engineer, one would know that a small part of the machine can understand so little of the scheme and the plan which are made for the working of the whole universe. If anybody understands this it is the awakened soul; but how much does he understand? Very little! And how does he understand it? He can only say that all justice and injustice, which may seem so to us on the surface, will all fit in and be perfect at the finish, where there is the summing up of the working of the whole universe. There is a saying in support of this in the 'Vadan':*

'When you stand on the earth and look at life, there is all injustice and chaos everywhere; but when you rise above and look below, it is all just and perfect, and everything appears to be in its proper place.' (Chala 76)

ON THE FEAR FOR DEATH

(to accompany pages 47 and 138)
22nd August, 1923, 3.30 p.m.

What is the meaning of the dizziness one feels when standing on a height?

The cause of it is expressive of a very great secret, the secret why there are many people who are afraid of spiritual truth. They would like to run away from the place where spiritual truth is spoken. I do not mean that they do not like the Church or God mentioned before them, or goodness. But if you tell them some secret about God, they want to run away: they get the same feeling as a person gets who

---

*When Hazrat Inayat Khan said this 'The Divine Symphony or Vadan' – collected aphorisms, poetically expressed ideas, chants and poems – was still a manuscript. Its first publication took place in 1926.

stands on the top of the mountain and looks below. They see such a gulf between them and God, they are afraid because they feel attraction.

Why does dizziness come? Because the earth attracts them. It is quite possible that that attraction might become so great that they would be without control or resistance and would jump down, because it is like a magnet which is attracting them with its power. A man holds himself back from it by force – not to jump! Wherever there is a gap and yet there is attraction, there is that feeling. I have often met people who, as soon as philosophical ideas were introduced, and the relation between God and man, got so afraid, that that feeling of dizziness came. It is because they cannot deny the truth of these ideas, but they want to save their life from the attraction. It is the fear of the gap, of the wide horizon which they are not accustomed to see.

But it is a matter of getting accustomed to it. There are builders of houses who stand on the highest top of a house – especially in America where they are working on scaffolds twenty or thirty storeys high – and from there look down and move about. They do not fear: they have become accustomed. It is exactly the same with the sages, the thinkers. The picture of the workman on high houses is the same as the picture of the sage who looks at what may be called life on the surface, and the eternal life. The gap between the two, which is death to others, becomes a bridge for him, uniting this life and the eternal life. The more he thinks of it, the less fear he has. There is a saying of a Sufi, 'The *Walī* has no fear of death.' He loses the fear of death.

[Question not recorded]

Whether a person is attracted by God now, or whether he is not attracted, there will come a day when he will be attracted, for everyone has to return to God.

Where does the fear of death come from?

APPENDIX

Ignorance of the self gives fear of death. The more one learns of the self, the less fear there is of death, for then man sees only a door to pass through from one phase of life to another – and the other phase is much better. The more spiritually one lives, the less fear there is of death. The more one lives in the soul, the less hold one has upon the body. The body has fear according to the consciousness it has in itself. Man is not only dependent upon his mind for thought, but every atom of the body is to some extent conscious, and so protects itself.

If that consciousness were raised high, and if it were shown the Light, the consciousness would know: this is a camp that I occupy; it is not my prison, it is my camp and I can leave it whenever I like. Man must learn to control his consciousness, and then he can raise it. When a person is conscious of headache, he feels his head ache; and when asleep, the condition of the head is the same; but in sleep the consciousness is removed and therefore he does not feel his head. If a person could collect his consciousness through will-power, as it automatically moves away in sleep, he would rise above pain. The degree of consciousness in the atoms is dependent upon the soul.

ON GOD'S JUSTICE

(to accompany pages 78 and 142)
10th September, 1923, 5.30 p.m.

Will you speak about the justice of God's judgment?

By giving you a little simile I will show you what difference there is between man's justice and God's justice: there are children of the same father and they are quarreling over their toys. They have reasons to quarrel over their toys. One thinks a certain toy is more attractive, why should he not possess it? The other says, that toy is given to him, why should he not hold on to it? Both have their reason and both are just, but the father's justice is different from theirs. The father has not only given them the toys to play with, but at the same time he knows what is the character of each child and what he wishes to bring out of that child, and whether that particular toy will help to bring out what he wishes to come out. The child does not know this. It happens, perhaps, that the toy seems poor to him and, according to his sense of justice, he cannot understand why that toy was given to him and not to the other. If the child was older, he would have accused the father of injustice! But he does not know the justice of his father; he has to grow to that stage of evolution where his father is, in order to understand the meaning behind it.

The same is with the justice of God and man. Man's justice is covered by his limited experience in life, by his favour and disfavour, by his preconceived ideas, by the learning he has, which is nothing compared with the knowledge of God. When one compares the father with his innocent child, their relationship is too near to be compared to the relationship between God and man, where there is such a distance. If we counted all the human beings that exist, they would be like a drop compared with the ocean. There is no comparison between God and man. Therefore man's justice is imperfect: God's justice is perfect.

If one ever gets a glimpse of divine justice, the only way is first to believe in the justice of God against all the proofs which will contradict His justice; there are many proofs which will contradict His justice. Why is this person rich, why is the other person poor, why is this person in a high position, why has that person suffered so much and why has another lived long and had a pleasant life? If one judged their actions, their intelligence, their stage of evolution, one would find no justification. By judging this, one will come to a conclusion where one will say, 'Oh, there is no justice, it is all a mechanical working which is perhaps behind it.'

APPENDIX

Ideas such as *karmā* and reincarnation will satisfy, but at the same time this will not root out God behind it. Then God has no power. God cannot be all-powerful, if everyone has the power to make his own *karmā*. Root out God, then everything is working mechanically. And if so, then there cannot be a machine without an engineer; for a machine there must be an engineer. Is he subjected to his machine? Is he subjected to its power, or the controller of it? If he is subjected, then he is not powerful enough. If he is limited, then he cannot be God any more. God is He, Who is perfect in His justice, in His wisdom and in His power.

If we question the cause of all such happenings which do not give us a justification, then we come to another question, and that question is: Can a composer give a certain justification for every note that he has written in his composition? He cannot, he can only say: 'It is the stream that has come from my heart. I have tried to maintain certain laws, to keep to certain rules of composition, but if you ask me for the justification of every note, I am unable to give it. I am not concerned with every note, I am concerned with the effect that the whole produces.'

It is not true that there is no law. There is a law; but is law predominant or love? Law is a habit, and love is the being. Law is made, love has never been created, it was, it is and it will be. So love is predominant. What do we read in the Bible? God is love. So God is beyond the law, love is above the law. Therefore, if we come to any solution to our ever rising question: why is it so? – it is not by the study of the law, never. Study of the law will only give increasing appetite, which will never bring satisfaction. If there is anything which will bring satisfaction, it is diving deep into love and letting love inspire law. That will open up a realm of seeing the law better.

Then we shall see that there is nothing in this world which has no justification. It is inexplicable, but it is perceptible that all has its justification, and in the light of perfect justice all life will be manifest. Then we shall not have one word to say that 'this is unjust', not even the most cruel thing we saw. A thing like this will shock, but at the same time this is the point the wise man reaches, and he calls it the culmination of wisdom.

ON DESTROYING THE PAST

(Continuation of page 84 and to accompany page 106)
28th August, 1923, 5.30 p.m.

WITH time it is the same thing as with the bodily form: it does not exist. All here is a play of shadows. In the sentence: 'I slept in the mineral, I stirred in the vegetable, I dreamed in the animal, I awoke in man', who is 'I'? It is God, Who says this.

Now there is the question of time from the human point of view. From the human point of view there is time, but from the spiritual point of view there is not.

The question that all souls have a sum total of difficulties which is the same, means: the sum total of their difficulties in the shadows. The only living moment in this world of shadows is the now. Past and future do not really exist.

But can the past be changed? Yes, it can, the past can be changed: that is the whole key to the understanding of this illusion. Two things have to be understood:

to use matter to its best advantage,

to rise above matter.

Why is the past dead? Because dead is that which does not have a real existence. The shadow is dead, not the light, the light has only disappeared.

Why does God live only in the moment of now and not in the past and in the future? Because God is eternal, and the life of the moment is His fullest experience.

The past can be changed by making oneself independent of its horrible effect. One must deny what one does not want to have. The secret is that only God's mind lives, and not the minds of mankind, which are doing acts of shadows. To live means for man his only chance to focus his mind on God's mind. The whole secret is that things which belong to the earth and things which belong to heaven cannot be compared. For instance, one moment of the djinn world is equal to a hundred years of this world, and a hundred years of the djinn world are equal to one moment of the angelic world. There is no comparison.

3rd July, 1923, 5.30 p.m.

If the past can be destroyed, what happens to the *ākāshic* records?

What is once created manifests and goes on manifesting. It requires a tremendous power to destroy what one has created; but the idea of the mystic is hidden in the word annihilation, which is not generally understood. Annihilation is really the art of the mystic.

Shiva is called the Destroyer. His power is considered greater than that of Brahma, the Creator. This subject takes man into one of the greatests mysteries. If there were no means of destroying, then the inharmonious elements would consume the whole creation. By means of destruction creation is restored; but one must know what to destroy. A Persian verse says, 'The master mind is that which knows what to destroy and what to restore.' The plants and trees have bugs and germs. These may be destroyed and the plant may be made better. So in the character of man, in his mind and thought there are things that may be destroyed. Many people hold fast the thought of illness for many years and in spite of all remedies they are still ill. Healing is the way of destroying these thoughts. True healing is the destruction of these thoughts.

4th July, 1923, 3.30 p.m.

As the whole of life is based on destroying, and the end – the fulfilment of all creation – will be destruction, what is meant by the Buddhistic law not to destroy?

The idea of the Buddhistic law not to destroy is that what should be maintained should be protected and preserved. People who are very destructive are destroying things which should be protected and preserved. So kindness and love is taught to people. People were taught to feel the pain of others, to sympathize with their suffering.

But one must remember that often, by destroying, one gives happiness. There are things that must be destroyed in order to produce happiness. There are sometimes thoughts, imaginations, feelings and impressions which must be destroyed. The master mind knows clearly what to destroy and what to protect, for to the master mind the whole world becomes a kind of garden. As the gardener knows what to destroy and what to keep, so the master mind knows what is to be protected and what is to be destroyed.

ON REINCARNATION

(To accompany pages 56 and 157)
Probable date: between 1916 and 1920

IT is argued that, because every soul is not worthy to be directly merged in God, it reincarnates numberless times in order to become perfect, until the final destination is reached, being bound to pay the penalty before reaching the presence of God.

The answer to this is, that if man in his limited sense of justice never punishes without stating why the punishment is given, how can it be supposed that God, the Merciful and Just, could cause a soul to reincarnate on earth as a penalty, without making him aware of his fault.

The scientific argument for reincarnation tells us that a seed sinks into the earth and produces other seeds and that this process is repeated thousands of times, the seed always becoming seed again. In this argument consists the possibility of reincarnation; for if the seed has sufficient strength to return as a seed, why should man's soul not re-don a human body?

APPENDIX

The answer is that even the seed, until it reaches the innermost culmination, is never able to spring up again as a seed. Besides, it cannot be called a reincarnation of the seed, but a regeneration. Again, one seed produces so many, therefore it cannot be called an incarnation, for the nature of incarnation would be one coming as one, but not one turning into many.

The same is the case with the soul which, after experiencing life independently through the medium of the world formed of the five elements, passes away off to its own source, carrying with it the impressions of the external world which it has gathered, dropping them at each step as it advances towards its own essence, the Universal Spirit. The earth substance passes into the earth, the water returns to water, the fire takes to its own element, the air bears away its own property and the ether does the same. When this frame of the five elements which, just like the burning glass, was able to receive the reflection of the spirit, is dispersed, the soul then takes its way to its original source where nothing remains of an individual after the bodily and mental frames are broken up. After this there is no chance of individuality, because there was none left but the Whole Being.

There are some who pretend, or at least imagine, to recollect their past, but in many cases they do so in order to create a sensation among people for the sake of notoriety, or in another case some give an expression to their whims and delusions.

The Yogis, who are the propounders of this idea, will not for one moment believe that reincarnation is for them. They claim *jīvan mukta* – free life. For those who cannot see anything but the objective world, the theory of reincarnation opens up to their imagination a vast field of interest and curiosity. Again, there are some who always look for something new; this desire goes to such an extent that even if a new God were produced, they would still seek for another God.

The truth of the reincarnation theory can be understood in one way: that there is a possibility that the self-same proportion of consciousness, which has once been a soul, may happen to form again as a soul, but in general there is no possibility. Just in the same way the self-same bubble may form a bubble again, but generally it is not so, for either half, quarter or even a hundredth part of the first bubble may group in other atoms of water, and quite another bubble may be produced. In both cases the soul has to merge into consciousness before it is sufficiently alive to manifest again. Therefore we cannot call it the same soul, because it is quite pure from its previous conditions. It is just like a drop of ink fallen into the ocean; the water merges into water and its inky substance sinks to the bottom, it never again remains as a distinct drop of ink, but is pure as the ocean. If it was again taken out from the water, it would no longer show its previous substance. Such is the nature of the soul when merged into the ocean of consciousness.

Of course, reincarnation is a very interesting subject to discuss and a good scope for the play of imagination. Therefore people have taken it up to awaken the curiosity of the masses who seek God with their scientific or mathematical attitudes. This subject specially interests those who cannot see any other than the objective life, and therefore do not want to get away from it. Their only consolation lies in imagining that they will come again.

It may appear by noticing the world's evolution that it is the soul which, owing to its previous experience in life, enables itself to manifest in a better condition than in the past. But in reality it is not so. The evolution of the world does not depend upon the soul's previous experience. But the cause why the world progresses at each step of evolution is that the soul partakes of the improved conditions upon its way towards manifestation, and thus helps manifestation to progress towards perfection.

The doctrine of reincarnation claims mostly its truth in the law of action which at once agrees with the intellect. That is to say: a man is a genius in music because of his past experience in it. If a person is lame and blind from birth, it is because of the penalty for past bad actions, which must be paid before he is purified. If a person is wise and spiritual, wealthy and powerful, it is because of his good actions in the past, which explains that every soul which does good or bad reaps its result through its reincarnations, until it arrives at its destiny.

The above doctrine may be contradicted by saying that it was not any fault of the legs which has caused them to bear the weight of the whole body. And it was not the head which did better in the past, which has made it to be the crown of the whole person. The world is the embodiment of One Being, God. The explanation of this can be found in the following quotation of a dervish, who said in Persian:

'Man is enjoying his belief in God, not knowing whether He is his friend or foe. It seems as if it were the ocean throwing up its waves joyfully, and a twig floating upon them thinks that it is for it that the ups and downs are caused by the ocean.'

Such is the case with all conditions in life. An individual thinks: 'I have done something in the past and that is why I am like this now, as it is the rule of God's justice'. But he is mistaken here. The ocean, like God, has many like him to think of and to judge, and therefore his rise and fall are either caused by Qaḍā*, the waves of the ocean of existence, or by that which his soul has gathered of good or evil while on the way towards manifestation.

The thinkers who have taught the doctrine of reincarnation have never meant it as it is understood by people in general. The reincarnation meant by them is as the partaking of the fresh soul descending towards manifestation, while the attributes of the souls which may be ascending toward their original source have given their impressions, or load of experience to the willing souls met with on the way.

The soul having once manifested as a body, never again has sufficient energy to manifest again. The idea of the soul reincarnating in another form has little truth in it. If it is true that the soul reincarnates as a matter of course, why not reincarnate in its original form, which it could easily have collected again?

(Summer 1924, dictated to Shaikh Sirdar van Tuyll)

Reincarnation exists for the personality, not for the ray. God works out His plan by making the personality reincarnate with a new ray. One personality is the reincarnation of another, and takes that other's problems where they were left.

The ray coming to earth chooses its own circumstances, its own personality to take up. On the foundation of this personality of the past it builds with the impressions from those around it a new personality. So – seen from the point of

---

* Qaḍā is the divine force that is working through all things and beings.

view of God – it is a reincarnation of an old personality, but from the point of view of the soul it is its own – not a reincarnation, but an incarnation.

All the experiences of the personalities are God's, and it is God Who works out in a series of reincarnations a problem which He brings by this to perfection.

There are two principal chains of cause and effect. The first plan is the cause and effect of the series of personalities. This is the law of the Vedanta school and it is illustrated by Christ's words: 'It is another who sows, and another who reaps.' Secondly there is the cause and effect for the soul, illustrated by Christ's words: 'Thou wilt reap as thou hast sown.' This leads the soul through heaven and hell to God.

The first is horizontal *karmā*, the second vertical *karmā*. But then there is a third form of *karmā*, a third chain of cause and effect. It is the Consciousness which stands as a gulf between the first two; it shows them distinctly as two different forms of *karmā*, and still it unites them. They are in union. One could call this inner *karmā*. It is imperceivable, incomprehensible: it belongs to God.

As to this third aspect, everyone is linked up with everyone else, and everyone can say he is a reincarnation of everyone from the past, as the universal Mind, from where the personality came, is One.

The secret of the soul is that it does not exist. Only God exists. God is God, God is the soul, and God is the chain of personalities.

27th August, 1923, 5.30 p.m. (continuation of page 78)

Is the doctrine of reincarnation not a missing link in the understanding of the attraction of the rays to the different kingdoms?

The other day I was very interested in San Francisco in the house of Murshida Martin★ to meet a Buddhist from Japan, a man who had about six thousand disciples in Japan. With him came a Theosophist who was a lecturer on Theosophy. I very much wanted this Buddhist to speak, and he

★ See 'The Biography of Pir-o-Murshid Inayat Khan'.

wanted me to speak. So the rivalry was so great that neither spoke. The Theosophist felt uncomfortable, because neither of us would speak, so he began to talk himself about the lectures he had given. But I wanted to hear something from the Buddhist and asked him: 'Will you please tell me something about Buddha?' He said: 'What is there to be told? The same truth, we call it Buddha. Perhaps you know Buddha better than I.'

[The Theosophist began to speak about reincarnation. I said to the Buddhist: 'What do you think about it?']★
He said: 'It is his Buddhism.' I wanted just to dig it up a little more and said: 'What? Do you mean to say that Buddha never taught reincarnation?' He said, 'I cannot say that. But what he taught us, we do not find any reincarnation in it. The people in India believe in reincarnation – he had to appeal to their mentality. Perhaps he spoke of reincarnation.' I said: 'But do you believe in reincarnation?' He said: 'It is the same truth, the same truth that you believe.'

Suffism is not against any particular doctrine. Why should it be against any doctrine? A message which has come to reconcile religions, must it oppose any doctrine? If you went to India, you would hardly find anyone speaking about reincarnation, and if one were to speak about it, he would speak on the moral of *karmā*. If you go to a Yogi, he will say, 'No, I am striving for *mukti*, for liberation. You want to be born again, therefore you will be born again. You would be very disappointed if you were not.' But it wants to be seen from a delicate point of view. To whom does he point you? He points you to what he knows to be 'you' in you.

I have never spoken against this doctrine, as I do not see the wrong of it, but neither do I see the right of it. When the purpose of life is realizing the unity

★There being a hiatus in the original records, this sentence cannot be vouched for.

of God, and losing from one's mind the false self, then the idea of reincarnation is based upon the conception of the false ego.

Sufism wants first to tell you what you are. As soon as you have solved what you are, there is no more question: what will my actions do for me? It is the question what you are that will solve the questions of reincarnation.

It is true that punishment comes from your bad actions. But what are you? And what actions will bring which result? Who can tell? What is apparent is different from what is hidden. Is a man who is born in a palace rewarded, or is the man who is perhaps starving in the street punished? I do not mean that the doctrine of reincarnation is wrong, but what is the right of it? It is based upon the false ego. Where is the right of something which is based upon the false ego, against which all religions have taught?

What has Christ taught? Salvation. What has Mohammed taught? *Najāt*, salvation. What did the Hindu Avatars bring? *Mukti*, salvation.

Therefore my idea is to wave it off and to keep before your vision the ideal of unity, the ideal in which we all unite, and in which is the fulfilment of life.

8th July, 1923, 5.30 p.m. (continuation of page 112)

What do you mean by 'the secret of reincarnation' as a doctrine of the Hindus. It did not explain *karmā*.

Karmā is another side of reincarnation. What I am saying is: why are some born as a genius in art, music, painting? Why are they born like this? The Hindus said: it is reincarnation of a great genius. Not only does the child inherit from the nation, the parents, the race, but also certain impressions are gained by the soul from some spirit as it passes through.

Is our coming on earth ruled by a law, or does it happen in a haphazard way?

APPENDIX

This very subtle problem is very difficult to explain. We are helped by understanding the meaning of accident and intention. They are two distinct things. It helps us if we try to discover what is hidden behind accident. Then we come to the intention in the scheme of the working of the whole.

Everything has a purpose, nothing is an accident; but to our mind there is accident. So accident exists for us like a shadow. Neither has shadow a real existence, nor has accident. Nothing is really accidental, but as the idea of accident goes on, it attracts accidents more and more. For instance, a person may wander for six months in Paris without finding a thief, but for a thief it will not take six hours to find one, for the law of attraction works. There is a verse in the Qur'an which explains this very well: 'Not one atom moves without the command of God.'

Intention is behind every activity, and the intention which we do not know, we call accident.

4th September, 1923 (asked and recorded by Shaikh Sirdar van Tuyll)

Murshid, can one say that those who believe in reincarnation are looking through green glasses and that they who are not believing in reincarnation look at the same truth through blue glasses?

Yes, that is so.

But Murshid, what kind of glasses are you looking through? The green ones or the blue ones?

Your Murshid is looking through white glasses.

APPENDIX

ON RESPONSIVENESS AND DISCIPLESHIP

(continuation of page 90)
31st August, 1923, 5.30 p.m.

THERE is a story of a Murshid. A murīd went for a long time to
the house of a Murshid and tried to develop spiritually; but
with all his enthusiasm and desire to advance he remained in
the same place. After a long time he said 'Murshid, I have
patience no longer. I have lived now a long time under your
guidance and I do not see any further; I am standing in the same
place as before.' The Murshid felt very embarrassed to hear
those words from him and most sad. He said, 'Look here, my
son, come with me.' The first thing they met in the street was a
mad dog. The dog was barking and howling, and trying to
bite everyone. The Murshid looked at the dog, and instantly
the dog became sane. He said, 'Look here, do you see the
change? If the glance of Murshid can do that to an animal who
is not accustomed to wisdom, what must it do for a human
being like you? But if your doors are closed, what can
Murshid's glance do? You are enthusiastic; you are eager; you
are willing; but you are not open.' It is the openness of the
heart, it is the response, the respondent attitude which is the
principle thing in pupilship. That is what makes one a disciple.
We can learn that by seeing the difference between the pebble
and the diamond. The pebble does not take the light of the sun,
the diamond does.

The question whether it is the favour or disfavour of the
teacher which enlightens the mureed, may be answered by
saying that that soul cannot be a Murshid, who favours and
disfavours. The first condition of being a Murshid is to favour,
to favour the friend and to favour the enemy. There is no lack
of favour if a person does not become enlightened. When the
rain falls, it falls upon all the trees, but according to the
response of those trees they grow and bear fruit. The sun
shines on all the trees: it does not make distinctions between
this tree or that tree, but in accordance with the absorption of
the light falling upon them and according to the response the
trees give to the sun, they get it.

Remember, at the same time, that very often a mureed is an

199

inspiration for the Murshid, because it is not the Murshid who teaches, it is God Who teaches. The Murshid is only a medium. As high as the response of the murīd reaches, so strongly does it attract the Message of God. The murīd can inspire and the murīd can shut off the inspiration too. If there is no response on his side, if there is antagonism on his side, if there is lack of interest on his side, then the inspiration of the Murshid becomes closed. Just like the clouds, when running over the desert, cannot shower. It is the desert which affects them. When the clouds come over the forest, the trees attract, and the rain falls.

ON THE SOUL'S JOURNEY DURING THE TIME
THE BODY IS ASLEEP

(to accompany page 93)
14th August, 1923, 3.30 p.m.

What does the soul do at night when the body sleeps?

Poor soul! Upon the soul there are so many demands. When the body is awake, then the soul must wander with the body wherever it will take it. When the body is asleep, the soul must go with the mind where the mind takes it, which is often farther than the body can. Of course, in this connection one must think of that sentence in the Bible, 'Where your treasure is, there your heart will be also.' It is not the heart, it is the soul that is meant. It is there where the treasure is. Is it in heaven, then the soul is in heaven; is it on earth, then the soul is on earth. If the treasure is in the purse, then the soul is in the purse. If it is in music, poetry, philosophy, thought, then the soul is with that.

All one admires, values, loves in life, the soul is with it. If one loves sadness, then the soul is in sadness; if one loves to experience joy, then the soul is joyous. What one seeks after, that is where the soul goes. Yet the soul touches all the spheres from the lowest to the highest. Even the soul of the most wicked person touches all spheres. Only he does not experience the benefit of it, because – when he is conscious – the soul is touching wickedness; and when the soul is unconscious while it touches the highest, what is the use?

The blessing of life is in the consciousness of the blessing. When one is not conscious of the blessing, it is nothing. If a kitten is privileged to sit on the sofa of the king and is dwelling all the time in Buckingham Palace, it is not really privileged, because it is not conscious of the privilege.

15th August, 1923, 3.30 p.m.

Will you give more particulars about the soul's journey during the time the body is asleep?

Either the soul is caught in the mind during sleep and it experiences the condition of the mind, or the soul enters the spiritual spheres where it is charged with inspiration, power and a new life. So when a person awakes, he feels inspired, rested, invigorated and very often blessed. A great load has been removed from his mind.

Does the soul sometimes have visits during the sleep of the body? Is it possible for a soul to visit another soul during the sleep of the body?

It is the soul of the other person being reflected in the soul of this person. Then two persons have the same experience and the knowledge of each other's condition.

Is it possible for one of the souls to help the other?

Yes, mostly one of those souls is advanced and has the power to help.

APPENDIX

ON MEDITATION

(to accompany pages 93 and 126).
28th August, 1923, 5.30 p.m.

Is meditation to be compared with growing in a hothouse?

Yes. Our life is so artificial that it gives us the need for meditation. If our lives were not so artificial we would not need meditation or religion. Every soul is born with the capacity to draw to it all the spiritual bliss and ecstasy that is necessary for its evolution. Ancient races who were not civilized had their own way of drawing that bliss. Also birds and animals have this way. If it were not so, it would be very unfair and unjust for the birds and animals that man should have that blessing and exaltation, and the birds and animals, who have done nothing wrong, should be deprived of it. But it is not so. We are deprived of it, because we have deprived ourselves of it. Nature gives all the bliss that is necessary for our soul; but having developed in ourselves such an unnatural way and habits of living, we cannot draw that bliss which the animals and birds can draw.

14th September, 1923, 3.30 p.m.

You once said that this Message would teach the labouring men to make from their labour their way of meditation. Will you please speak more on this subject?

I had meant that the chief work of this Message is to make man's everyday life a religion, his profession his religion, his work his religion. Whatever he is capable of doing he must do it and at the same time, while doing it, he can meditate on that work by knowing the sacred meaning of that work he is doing, in this way turning his life, the same life, from a worldly life into a spiritual life. While doing the work for which he is qualified and needed, he will be accomplishing his religion and he will attain spirituality by his meditation on the evolution of his work, however unimportant, as soon as he knows how to do the meditation in the right way.

Even the man in the factory making bottles?

Even he. Whether he is doing gardening or factory work, as soon as he knows the meditation of the work he is doing, then his work becomes a meditation for him.

Of course the man in the factory has not the same facility as the one who is doing gardening, for nature is a bliss. Still for him, whatever he does, if he attaches to it this thought of meditation, his wages will be nothing compared with the bliss he gets. So his sacrifice is no loss, when he understands this.

Would not the work suffer? Can one think of something else while meditating?

There is no other thing to think about. When the right teaching is given, a person is doing his work in the right way and even better than the other people, because his mind will be concentrated.

I shall tell you my own experience. Once I came to a station in Rajputan and I had to send a telegram. I saw a telegraph clerk taking the telegram, doing the work and yet doing his meditation at the same time. It interested me very much: a man as busy as that, who had to listen every time to the bell of the telegraph while doing his work. A mistake of one letter would hold him responsible. He came to me and I said, 'I have come to give you this telegram, but I marvel at you. It is wonderful how you are keeping your meditation during this work.' He looked at me and smiled and instantly we became friends and had an interesting talk afterwards.

If this were not possible, the spiritual work would be a nuisance, especially in times when life's need is so great that everybody has a certain work to do and very few hours rest. If a person thinks that after having reached a certain age he will have leisure, then the whole life is wasted. The best method, therefore, is to use the way of meditation in one's everyday life.

Whatever one does, must be done with meditation. It will be done properly, and one will not only have the benefit of the earth, but also from heaven. One will get the wages a thousand times over, the benefit will be a thousand times greater.

What is meditation in this sense?

Meditation means the soul's endeavour towards spiritual unfoldment. This endeavour may be practised in different ways, in order to suit one's own profession and work.

14th September, 1923, 5.30 p.m.

Is the person who communicates many hours a day with God nearer to Him than the one who must concentrate on his duties without the chance of communicating definitely?

One must make one's duties a religion and find a means of communication through one's everyday life. If the Sufi Message has to bring anything to the world, it is this. By the meditations and concentrations which are given to the murīds, it is not meant that this is the only means for them to communicate with God. This is a way, this is a key. From this way they must develop and learn how to communicate with God in all things they do in their life. It is not sufficient to sit for half an hour or an hour in the thought of God. Every moment of our life must be devoted to it.

I remember the words of my Murshid, answering my question on sin and virtue. He said: 'There is one sin and one virtue. The moment which is passed in the absence of God is sin and every moment of life which is passed in the presence of God is virtue.' The object of the whole work in the Sufi culture is that we arrive at a stage in our life that – after having learned this way of concentration – we are at every moment of our life in communion with God. When we are talking with others, when we are walking, sleeping, in every action we do, God must be before us.

Is that within everyone's reach?

We are meant to be so. Just think, when a person is in love with someone, he is capable of thinking of the same person all the time; while eating, drinking, walking, the image of the beloved is there. That shows that man is capable of it. When the same love is developed for God, it is natural to think at every moment of our life of God in all we do.

ON THE SUFI AND THE YOGI

(continuation of page 109 and to accompany page 93)
4th July, 1923, 5.30 p.m.

Will you tell us more about the Sufi training and that of the Yogis?

The Yogis of ancient times had one training only, the training of the head centre, to make the sight keen and the perception deep; but the training of the heart is the Sufi method. The training of *bhakti* came among the Yogis from the time of Krishna. The Sufi has always considered that training of head and heart gave balance in life. In India, if one visits the places of the great Yogis, the atmosphere and the impression that one gets in their presence is very strong. The impression is that everything is wortheless and nothing is worth while in life. They desire only one thing and that is to get away from it, and by getting away from it to get above it. This makes one feel that one does not wish to remain one moment in this world. One wants to go to the caves and forests and pass one's whole life in the eternal peace, the only true bliss and happiness there is. Then there is the feeling in the presence of the Yogi as if nothing exists, not even trees, plants, birds.

APPENDIX

The overwhelming influence of the Yogi is such that the person feels for the moment that he is blind and deaf to the whole world. He feels only the one eternal Being; with him all else is non-existent, and in his presence one may even come to the point where one does not know any existence at all.

In the presence of the Sufi one feels the atmosphere of love, kindness, affection, service, sociability, friendliness, because the central theme of the Sufi is God, his Beloved. So he lives in the presence of his Beloved, and love he considers as life. So in his presence one has the feeling of fullness, of joy and of the fragrance of roses, of incense, bringing ecstacy with joy. Many in disappointment, heartbroken and in trouble go into the presence of the Sufi and from his word, his glance, his silence, his atmosphere get courage to fight on, courage to look forward to life. If it is not good now, it will be better tomorrow. If he does not understand now, he will tomorrow. That which he cannot attain now, tomorrow will be attainable. A Sufi has always hope, because – while the idea of the Yogi begins with the object of losing his self and living in the perfection of God – the Sufi first begins his journey to perfection in the human soul; and this the Sufi considers the fulfilment of his coming upon earth. After accomplishing this, the other thing which the Yogi strives for, does not come with so much difficulty. He can then easily attain that ideal which is one step further. In this way the Sufi fulfils the first step in experiencing the perfection of the human soul. A second step is to learn the perfection of the Being of God.

To one the Yogi part is more akin, but as far as I can see, I think that to many the part of the Sufi appeals most. Imagine, if all were to leave the world and go to the caves and forests in order to become wise, then what would the world be without any of the wise? The power of the Yogi is such that his presence is an intoxication. To the Indian temperament the Yogi method appeals much.

APPENDIX

Vairāgya is very dear to the people of India. The very presence of the Yogi convinces many of the futility of life.

17th September, 1923, 3.30 p.m.

What is the Sufi idea of the cross and of expansion?

The way of the Yogi is to work in order to dive deep within himself, and so to pass through all the different planes which stand between himself and God, the Self within. The way of the Sufi is the way of expansion. As he draws within, so he widens his outlook on life so that in the end, when he has touched the innermost part of his being, he has embraced almost all that is living.

It is this idea which is pictured by the sign of the cross. Reaching to one's innermost being is signified by the perpendicular line, and the expansion which widens man's outlook on life is signified by the horizontal line. Therefore the cross in the end becomes the heart-round, but the circle does not show the two aspects in their essence as the heart shows. When one sees in the centre of the heart, it shows to the mind with keen imagination the perpendicular line and it gives also an idea of the horizontal line. The difference between the circle and the heart is that the circle, which expresses the cross, is the heart. Leaves are of heart-shape rather than round, and the veins of the leaf show the cross.

One sees in the life of Sufis and Yogis this difference. The Yogi's attitude is keeping everyone away, at a distance. He will bless, but he will bless a person from a distance and say kindly: 'Don't come near'. He does not hate, but he would rather be left alone.

The Sufi, on the contrary, comes with open arms to welcome all who come, for in every person he sees the spark of the divine Being. Therefore he becomes all-embracing. In this way he widens his outlook.

APPENDIX

ON KAMAL

(to accompany page 141 – note 60 –)
21st August, 1923, 3.30 p.m.

If *kamāl* is inertia, does everything have a moment of rest regularly, and if so, how often?

The rest between life and the hereafter is what is called purgatory. There is always a gap between two actions. For instance, when a person takes two steps, there is a gap between them. Between inhaling and exhaling there is a gap. Therefore in every breath there is a moment of *kamāl*. Then in the breathing of every day, after three quarters of an hour, there comes a short time when the breath changes and at that time also there is a *kamāl*. It is for this reason that there are certain times during the day when a person feels lazy, depressed, or confused, for that is the outcome of *kamāl*. He has no tendency to action and sometimes certain days come in a week when a person with all his enthusiasm does not like to work. That is also *kamāl*.

But in some people's life *kamāl* obsesses them. They feel that they are against an iron wall. They don't see the way and everything seems to them still, no movement anywhere. It is a deplorable state. Many people mentally reach that state of *kamāl*, which continues within them and in the end results in a kind of insanity; an insanity of the worst kind, because that person wants to take his life. He has no interest in life, no desire to do anything. In other forms of insanity, when a person wants to fight, to kill someone, to do something, then there is hope for him. If they want to do something then there is hope. The cause of the first insanity is disorder of the breath. If such a person could breathe rightly, he would be cured. If someone could bring about balance between *jalāl* and *jamāl*, he would be cured.

APPENDIX

Is there a good kind of *kamāl*, to which sages reach?

That *kamāl* is a balance in breathing. When the sage brings about *kamāl* he switches off the activity of the mind at the time when he does not need to feel enthusiasm. He does it through his will when he needs a time of quiet.

The ordinary person, when he feels this inertia, must not give in. It is like death for the mind, and the world has so many beautiful things in poetry, music, nature. But when it comes to an active person then it can be right to give in to it, for it is then rest, sleep, relaxation to the active mind.

12th September, 1923, 5.30 p.m.

Will you please tell us if it is possible for us to guard against the moments of *kamāl* in which accidents happen?

No, one must not trouble about it, because the thought of an accident attracts accidents. It is best not to trouble about it. In order to avoid such accidents the best thing is to keep tranquil, for all accidents come when the tranquillity of the mind is disturbed. If one keeps one's mind in proper balance, no accident will come. An accident always follows the broken rhythm of the mind. When the mind has lost its rhythm, then there is an accident.

'But', you may say, 'when a person has a motorcar accident, is it his fault or the fault of the chauffeur?' The answer is: 'May be it is the fault of the chauffeur, may be it is his fault. His mind has upset the chauffeur or someone else too. The accident might come from another motorcar, and might also be reflected by his mind.' No one can blame the other, because we don't know. An accident is not natural; it is something unnatural and something undesirable.

For instance, the false note and the lack of rhythm are not intended by the composer; he did not mean that. When a person plays this, it is a mistake, it is not a desire.

CHRONOLOGICAL TABLE

NOTES

(Words placed in the quotations between brackets [] are added by the editor)

1. Definitions of some of the Eastern words used in the text of this Introduction have been given at greater length by the author in other of his works. The first definitions given below are to be found in 'A Sufi Message of Spiritual Liberty' – Chapter 'Manifestation' – the further descriptions are borrowed from an unpublished document from the archives of the 'Nekbakht Stichting' Foundation – Ref. No 20, 3206–.

Ahadiyyah: 'Plane of Eternal Consciousness.'
'The knowing faculty without the knowledge of anything, the Single Being.'

Wahdah: 'Plane of Consciousness.'
'That state where the Consciousness opens its eyes and realizes: I exist. *Wahdah* means singleness. This plane is *Wahdah* because, although it has lost the absolute aspect of its being, yet it has not before it any such object that it may realize that there are two, or that it may compare one with the other. Neither is it away from its original existence, nor is this part experiencing the same calm and peace which the original existence experiences. The difference between the original state and this one is that the original state is in its everlasting state of calm and peace, and the Consciousness which experiences sound has before it an attraction more intense in character, devoid of the calm and peace of its original state and confused with the experience which had a beginning, and will surely have an end. The indulgence of *Wahdah* with the sound forms a link between them, for it is the offspring of the same; therefore there is attachment.'

Wahdaniyyah: 'Plane of abstract ideas.'
'Being ceases to be single. In other words, its calm and peace is disturbed by its activity which is its nature. The nature of activity is that one part is active, as – when a person is active – the hand or foot is active, not the whole. The nature of activity is to produce sound, therefore the first activity that the Consciousness realizes is sound. Activity has a certain scope; therefore the Whole Being, hearing the sound, is attracted to it, is drawn into it. Thus its oneness is disturbed. The vibrations clashing with one another produce light, a still greater attraction for the Consciousness.'

Arwāh: plural form of the Arabic word *rūh* – spirit.
'The spiritual plane.'
'The nature of sound and light is to encircle, to encompass the Consciousness forming numberless circles, all grouped together. The Consciousness would seem like a Sun shining through a thousand holes, manifesting through each as a separate Sun. The attraction to the sound and light of the Consciousness – which is surrounded by

213

NOTES

them – is so great that, although the nature of the Consciousness is to meet with its other part, still it is so encircled by the law of attraction that it sticks fast.'

Ajsām: plural form of the Arabic word *jism* – body.

'The astral plane.'

'The nature of both, sound and light, making each of them creative and responsive, generates peculiar qualities and merits, faculties and inclinations, which form the mind, the thinking body. This plane is called *Ajsām*.'

Insān: 'The human kingdom.'

'These numberless *ajsām* [bodies], manifesting still more concretely in the objective world, turn into physical existence, the perfection of which is man, *Insān*.'

2. *Akāsha* – A Sanskrit word meaning sky.

Asmān – A Persian word meaning sky.

Cf. Inayat Khan in 'Philosophy, Psychology, Mysticism' – Chapter 'Capacity'–:

'The sky is a capacity. The capacity is that which makes a hollow, in which the action of the all pervading Existence may produce a substance . . . As the sea is a capacity in which all the animals of the water are born, live and die, so the air is a capacity in which many beings live and move and have their being, so the earth is a capacity which conceives in itself the plants, the trees and all the different stones and metals, minerals and different substances which come out of it. Again, everything – the stone or the tree, or a fruit, or a flower – is a capacity [e.g.] for a perfume, for a sweet savour to be formed there. And so the living being is a capacity, and man is a finished capacity. The Hindus name the capacity *ākāsha*. What is generally thought is that *ākāsha* means sky; but in reality *ākāsha* means everything.'

3. The Law of Vibration:

Cf. Inayat Khan in 'The Mysticism of Sound' – Chapter 'Vibrations'–

'It is the gradually increasing activity which causes vibrations to materialize, and it is the gradual decrease of the same which transmutes them again into spirit. As has been said, vibrations pass through five distinct phases while changing from the fine to the gross, and the elements of ether, air, fire, water and earth – each has a savour, colour and form particular to itself . . . At each step in their activity they vary and become distinct from each other; it is the grouping of these vibrations which causes variety in the objective world . . . Vibrations turn to atoms and atoms generate what we call life; thus it happens that their grouping by the power of nature's affinity forms a living entity . . . They make different forms, figures and colours as they shoot forth, one vibration creating another, and thus myriads arise out of one. In this way there are circles under circles and circles over circles, all of which form the universe.'

4. *Tanzīh and Tashbīh:*

Tanzīh: remoteness, the assertion of God's transcendance by denying all similarity.

NOTES

Tashbīh: comparison, the assertion of God's immanence with the help of symbols.

Cf. Inayat Khan's 'Biography': '*Tanzih* and *Tashbih* – entity and identity.'

Cf. also 'A Sufi Message of Spiritual Liberty' – Chapter 'Manifestation'– '*Aḥadiyyah, Waḥdah, Waḥdāniyyah* are *Tanzīh; Arwāḥ, Ajsām, Insān* are *Tashbīh.*'

5. Cf. Jelaluddin Rumi – a Sufi mystic poet (1207–1273) in his poem Mathnavi, Book I, verse 838:
'Air, earth, water and fire are God's servants. To us they seem lifeless, but with God they are living beings.'

6. In his lecture Hazrat Inayat Khan said 'omnipotent Light' and this was reproduced in the first edition of 'The Soul-Whence and Whither'. In the second revised edition this was however altered into 'omnipresent Light'.

7. Shams-e-Tabriz was a dervish Sufi mystic, who became the spiritual guide of Jelaluddin Rumi. Rumi's 'Diwan of Shams-e-Tabriz' is dedicated to him.
In several of his earlier lectures Inayat Khan quoted this verse as follows:
'When the sunfaced One had arisen, each atom of the two worlds appeared.
When the light of His face sent its shadows, by this shadow various names became.
The things – what were they? The picture of the names.
The atoms – what were they? He in reality.
The waves – what are they? They are in reality the sea.'

8. These two sentences keep more closely to Hazrat Inayat Khan's originally spoken words. Later they were partially altered; a new sentence was added and published in all subsequent editions: 'There arises a conflicting condition or entanglement of the Breath of God, disorder in its rhythm, which manifests in destruction and culminates in what is called by Hindus *pralaya*, the end of the world.'
The conception of the 'entanglement of the Breath of God' and the 'disorder in its rhythm' introduces a new idea which is not elaborated further in this book.

9. Hazrat Inayat Khan always distinguishes birds from other animals. In answer to a question about this he explained: 'One takes the direction of the sky. That direction itself makes it a different being. The other has the direction of the earth, which makes its inclination quite different.' (*8th September, 1924*)

10. Brahma and Shiva are the first and third Persons of the Hindu Trinity: God the Creator and God the Destroyer. The second Person is Vishnu, God the Preserver.

11. By 'the Prophet' is always meant the Prophet Mohammed.

12. '*Arsh:*
In his lecture Hazrat Inayat Khan said: '. . . make around this divine

NOTES

Spirit which is called *Nūr* by the Sufis an aura which is called the highest Heaven.'

'*Arsh* is the Divine Throne often mentioned in the Qur'an.

Nūr means light and is mostly used in this sense throughout this book, cf. pages 26, 38, 54 and 108. On page 9 it is used for "divine Spirit" and on page 10 for "ether".

13. Cf. page 20: '*asura* means lifeless, in other words, not in tune with the infinite.' This sentence is a revision of the original words spoken in the lecture: '*asura* means lifeless, in other words mortals [i.e. beings] whose life has been caught in the net of mortality.'

14. Jelaluddin Rumi's quotation that appears here is from the Mathnavi (verse 6).

'Hearken to the flute and listen to what it says.
It complains of the pain of separation.
It says: Ever since I have been cut apart from my bamboo stem
My cry has set man and woman weeping.
The heart would be torn to pieces by yearning
If I explained the agonies of pain in longing.
Everyone who is far from his own element
Seeks reunion with his own.
Everyone was drawn to me to become my friend
But none devined what it was in my heart that drew him.'
(From 'Love Human and Divine' by Sherifa Lucy Goodenough)

15. In 'Love Human and Divine' this story is told with many more details and names, and a more complete explanation of its symbolical meaning is given there.

16. Cf. Inayat Khan's 'The Unity of Religious Ideals' – Chapter 'The Spiritual Hierarchy':

'According to the Sufi conception there are several degrees distinguished as different stages of responsiveness [to God], in other words of higher initiation . . . *Walī* is the initiate whose will has come close to the divine will . . . He controls a community keeping it on the right track . . . *Ghawth* is the next grade of the initiates. The influence of the *Ghawth* is wider. He gives up his personality wholly to the divine guidance . . . He helps the spiritual wellbeing of a community . . . The *Quṭb's* mind becomes focussed to the divine mind . . . He governs spiritually a country or a nation . . . *Nabī* is the apostle whose spirit reflects the Spirit of Guidance. He elevates individuals and bears a divine Message . . . *Rasūl* is the world Messenger. Answering the cry of humanity he fulfills the purpose of his mission on earth.'

17. *Munkir and Nākir:* These Arabic words are both formed from the root *nakara* (the 'm' being a prefix) meaning: ignore, refuse to acknowledge, reprove. This explains the remark 'there is little difference in their names'. The sentence was omitted from previous editions.

18. *Jalāl – Jamāl:* Cf. Inayat Khan in 'The Mysticism of Sound' – Chapter 'Vibrations':

'The intensity of activity produces strong vibrations named in Sufi terms *jalāl*; the gentleness of activity causes mild vibrations called *jamāl*. The former activity works as strength and power, the latter as beauty and grace.'

19. *Nafs:* Cf. Inayat Khan in 'Philosophy, Psychology, Mysticism' – Chapter 'The Realization of the True Ego':
    'The process of mystical development is the annihilation of the false ego in the real ego. Sufis term the ego *nafs*, and the real ego is named by the Sufis Allah or God. It does not mean that the false ego is our ego, and the true ego is the ego of God. It only means that the true ego, which is the ego of the Lord, has become a false ego in us . . . The soul which comes from the highest source, having identified itself with a smaller domain, the domain of the body and mind, has conceived in itself a false idea of itself, and it is that false idea which is called *nafs*.'

20. Cf. page 46.
    'Even at the cost of all the happiness in heaven the soul touches the utmost point. Manifestation in the human form is the utmost border of the manifestation, the farthest one can go.'
    Cf. also page 57, the 3rd question – answer.

21. See the Illustration, page 172.

22. 'the nature of this current is to envelop in itself all that may come along'.
    These are the original words Hazrat Inayat Khan spoke in his lecture. In the subsequent editions they were shown as: '. . . to envelop itself with all that may come along'.
    Both descriptions are valid. Cf. page 53: 'all is collected and gathered upon the current which is within and that current is the soul.'

23. Cupid – mentioned on page 43 and on page 71 – is the soul which, wishing to manifest on the human plane, brings man and woman together in order that they may 'open the way for this new coming soul to enter physical existence'.

24. *Ṭawq:* We do not know whether this is the word Hazrat Inayat Khan meant to say. In the only available document that mentions it, it is spelt '*tok*'. The Arabic word '*ṭawq*' signifies the collar put around the neck of a dog. The word may also have been used to indicate the servitude of a slave.

25. The first and second editions of 'The Soul-Whence and Whither' substituted the word '*genius*' for the word '*djinn*'.
    Hazrat Inayat Khan nearly always used the word '*djinn*' in his lectures. (In the last two lectures of the series 'Towards the Goal' the word '*genius*' occurs three or four times.) He mostly used the word '*genius*' in the sense of an exceptional capacity of the mind. See e.g. page 48 and page 56.
    In 'The Sufi Message of Hazrat Inayat Khan', Volume I, the word '*jinn*' is used.

26. Indra is to the Hindus the King of Gods. Indra – loka is the world of Indra, Heaven. *Gandharvas* and *Apsaras* in the Hindu mythology are a class of demi-gods, who are the musicians and dancers in Indra's Heaven.

27. 'It is through this current that the fruit is connected with the stem' –

NOTES

These are the original words spoken by Hazrat Inayat Khan in his lecture. In subsequent editions they are shown as: 'It is through this branch that . . . *etc.*'

Cf. page 30: 'The soul of the prophet . . . is a link between heaven and earth; it is a medium by which God's Message can be received.'

Cf. also page 33: 'Devas – are as a fruit dropped on the earth but still connected with the branch. The branch has bent and the fruit has touched the earth, but it has not lost connection with the stem.'

28. Hazrat Inayat Khan spoke these words after the questions and answers following one of his lectures on 'Character Building' – 22nd August, 1923, 3.30 p.m. – They are published in this edition because they introduce the next chapter where the soul is compared to an electric current.

29. This paragraph is given here for the first time with all the words that were omitted from the previous editions. Even so it is still difficult to grasp the sense of the teaching, because different pictures are used to explain it.

1) First there is the whole manifestation which is the Breath of God, shooting forth, so to speak, in various breaths: the souls.

2) Then a similar picture appears in the Yogi conception of one central breath, *prāna*, branching out into various lesser breaths. This explains why Hazrat Inayat Khan says: 'These souls, *therefore*, are different breaths of God' – i.e. because they stand in the same relation to God's Breath as do the lesser breaths to *prāna*.

As the lesser breaths + *prāna* make one breath, *which we call life*, so the breaths that are souls + God's Breath make also one Breath – a divine Breath *which is Life*.

3) Finally appears the picture of the tree: the stem is God's Breath, or the manifestation: each branch is a soul, a *prāna*, which in its turn is as a stem to lesser branches, the lesser breaths.

30. Shankarachārya lived in the beginning of the ninth century. Exponent of the Advaita Vedanta, he is one of the greatest philosophers of India, declaring the oneness of God, the soul and the universe.

One of his poems: 'Six stanzas on Nirvana' ('Nirvanashatkam') repeats in each refrain: 'I am Shiva, I am Shiva' (Civoham).

31. Asif was the pen-name of Mir Maheboob Ali Khan, Nizam of Hyderabad, mentioned in the 'Biography of Pir-o-Murshid Inayat Khan'.

Some of his poems were published in 'Hindustani Lyrics'.

32. A seemingly obscure passage followed this sentence and was included in former editions of this book. Hazrat Inayat Khan actually said: 'These three planes, which are the principal planes of existence, are called in the terms of Vendanta *trilok*, which means three worlds: *bhu-lok.*, meaning physical world, *gāndhārva-lok*, meaning the world of *djinns*, and *dēva-lok*, the world of angels.'

In the first edition of the book this became: 'These three planes, which are the principal planes of existence, are called in the terms of Vedanta: *Bhu-*

loka, Dēva-loka, Sura-loka, meaning three worlds. *Bhu-loka* the physical world, *Dēva-loka* the world of the Genii, and *Sura-loka* the world of the angels'.

In spite of the correction proposed by Miss L. Goodenough: *Svar-loka* instead of *Sura-loka,* the above text was republished in the 2nd edition. The Barrie & Rockliff edition, Volume I, carries the same text as the 1st edition, but corrects *Sura-loka* to read *Svar-loka.*

According to authoritative Vedantic publications these terms – even the corrected ones – do not seem to correspond with the three spheres described in this work. Two questions and answers exchanged next day *(29th August, 3.30 p.m.)* on this subject add to the impression of uncertainty:

Question: The Vedanta speaks of 14 *lokas.* What is *loka?*

Answer: These 14 planes of existence are a conception of metaphysics. The Sufis call them *Choudatabaq,* 14 different experiences which the consciousness has by the help of meditation.

Question: Are those *lokas* divided into 7 planes?

Answer: These 14 planes have nothing to do with the angelic and the *djinn* planes; they are not divided into angelic or *djinn* planes, but in the experience of these 14 planes the *djinn* plane and the angelic plane and also the plane of the human being are touched.

See also 'The Way of Illumination' – Chapter 'Some Esoteric Terms', which describes *Choudatabaq* as 'the world unseen' and as 'the fourteen planes consisting of the seven heavens and the seven earths'.

33. Cf. Inayat Khan's 'Character-Building, The Art of Personality', consisting of two series of lectures given on the same days as his lectures on 'The Soul–Whence and Whither'.

Asked what difference there was between 'personality' and 'individuality', he answered (11th September, 1923, 3.30 p.m.):

'Individuality is the consciousness of the soul of its oneness, in spite of its various possessions with which it still identifies itself. The moment one says "I", one becomes conscious of an individuality, in spite of having different organs of the body and different thoughts, in spite of knowing: this is my hand, this is my foot, this is my head. It is seeing one's various parts, but with the tendency of attributing to oneself all the different parts and yet realizing "I am one", in spite of being many. Individuality is the realization that "in spite of being many, I am one". In plain words: I am one, composed of many aspects.

Personality is a development, an improvement of the individuality. When an individuality becomes a person, that beauty which is hidden in an individual and which is divine develops, and it is the development of that beauty which is personality. What we express from our selves, is an improvement of what we are. Individuality is nature, personality is art.'

34. Hazrat Inayat Khan's original words were: 'The law that attracts souls from the *djinn* world to the human world is all that they receive from the souls who are homeward bound.' The gifts that the soul receives in the *djinn* sphere oblige it – as by a law – to take a certain direction in its earthly life.

NOTES

Cf. page 55: 'This latter [the spirit on the return journey] gives the map of the journey to the soul travelling towards manifestation. It is from this map that the travelling soul strikes its path, rightly or wrongly.'

35. For a further explanation of this idea see page 82, the 2nd question – answer and page 158/159.

36. Cf. page 73/74.

37. 'Therefore the soul becomes susceptible to all influences . . . of that sphere from which it seeks its sustenance, which means the sustenance of the shell'. This seems to be the most logical version. However, according to several reports Hazrat Inayat Khan's spoken words were: 'Therefore that shell becomes susceptible to all influences . . . of that sphere from which it seeks its sustenance . . . ' Subsequent editions kept the word 'shell' and changed the words 'which means' into 'or rather'.

38. Cf. Jelaluddin Rumi, Mathnavi I, verses 388–392.
'Every night thou freest our spirits from the body
And its snare, making them pure as rased tablets.
Every night spirits are released from this cage,
And set free, neither lording it nor lorded over.
At night prisoners are unaware of their prison,
At night kings are unaware of their majesty.
Then there is no thought or care for loss or gain.
No regard to such a one or such a one.
The state of the knower is such as this, even when awake.'
(Translated by E.H. Winfield, London, 1898)

39. It was originally intended to include the following chapter in the book, but in the end it was left out. Its subject is the distinction of the five principal stages of evolution of the ego, *nafs*, which result from what the soul inherits from its passage through the different planes. If the chapter shows some resemblance with the next one, which distinguishes four classes of human beings from the point of view of their earthly heritage, the way the subject is developed is very different. This amply justifies its place in the present book.

40. Cf. page 125: '. . . Intelligence and soul are not two things; it is only a condition of the Intelligence which is the soul.'
Cf. also the definition of Intelligence given in 'The Way of Illumination': 'Intelligence is the grasping faculty of Consciousness which – by every means – recognizes, distinguishes, perceives, and conceives all that is around and about it.'

41. Kabir (1440–1518) was an Indian mystic and poet from Benares. Born a Muslim, he was accepted by a Hindu Guru and in his poems was able to fuse Islamic and Vedantic mysticism. His poems have been translated by Rabindranath Tagore, who revealed them to the Western world.
The poem Hazrat Inayat Khan refers to is probably the following:
'It is the mercy of my true Guru that has made me to know the unknown.
I have learnt from him to walk without feet, to see without eyes,
to hear without ears, to drink without mouth, to fly without wings.'

42. The Word that Was Lost:

NOTES

Inayat Khan has explained this subject in a lecture dated Dec 1922:
'. . . It is the work of the biologist to explain the details of the gradual development of the creation. The outline which the mystics of all ages have drawn, is that first there was the creation of the mineral kingdom, then that of the vegetable, then that of the animal kingdom, and finally that of man; and further, that through all this process of development there has been a certain purpose which has led the creation on towards the fulfilment of a definite object. But when the seer studies the whole sequence, mineral, vegetable, animal, and man, he finds something missing and reappearing as development proceeds. What is it that was missing? It is the expression and perception. It is this which the mystic referred to in the symbolic expression 'The Word that was lost'.

What made them say that 'the Word was lost'? It was that the Word was in the beginning; there was movement and vibration, there was the consciousness of the Perfect Being. The rocks were not made, even from a scientific point of view, before vibration manifested: vibration first, rocks afterwards. The difference between the mystical and the scientific point of view is only this, that the latter says that from the rock, by a gradual process, Intelligence developed, whereas the mystic will say: 'No, the rock was only a grade of Intelligence, Intelligence was first, and the rock came afterwards.'

The whole process of manifestation suggests that it is working towards some objective, and that objective is one and the same. One may look at it from two points of view. On the one hand one may say: 'A mountain will some day turn into a volcano, or a tree will bear fruits some day, and so the objective of each of them is fulfilled.' The other point of view is that the stones and trees and animals and men are all working towards one objective and the whole manifestation is working towards it. What is that purpose towards which every aspect of creation is working? What is it that the silent mountains are waiting for in the wilderness? What is it that the woods and trees are waiting for? What moment? What object? What is it that the animals are seeking and searching for (besides food)? What is it that gives importance to man's every activity, and draws him on to another when one activity is fulfilled? It is one object, though covered under many forms. It is the search after that Word, the Word that was lost. The further the creation develops, the more greatly does it long to hear this Word.

But as there is a gradual process from the mineral to the human kingdom, so there is a gradual process from a certain state of human evolution to a state of perfection. What is it that gives man the inclination to hear a word of admiration, a word of praise which satisfies him? What is it that pleases him when he hears the voice, the word of his friend? What is it that charms him in music, in poetry, and gives him joy? It is the same Word that was lost, appearing in different forms. Creation – I mean material creation – in its beginning seems to be deaf and dumb. Who feels this pain which comes from realizing it is deaf and dumb? It is that Spirit of perfection which has been perfect in perception and expression. The explanation of the soul which the great poet Jelaluddin Rumi gives in his Mathnavi expresses this idea in a poetical form. He says the soul is like a

NOTES

bird in a cage, deprived of that freedom and that joy which it was accustomed to experience. This also explains the main tragedy of life. Although every man, every soul suffers pain to a certain degree and will describe the cause of that pain differently, yet beneath the different causes there is one cause, and that cause is the captivity of the soul: in other words, that the Word was lost. . . . '

43. If we consider it from the point of view of the body and its senses, perception may seem to be a receptive quality. Hazrat Inayat Khan describes perception from a spiritual point of view, that of the soul: the soul expresses itself through the organs of perception of the body. Cf. Hazrat Inayat Khan in 'Philosophy, Psychology, Mysticism' – Chapter 'Intelligence': 'If human intelligence were to be defined, it could be divided into three aspects: perception, conception, assimilation. One is expressive, the other receptive and the third is all powerful'.

44. Cf. page 131/132: 'A certain satisfaction comes from having put into an objective form that which was first on another plane. It is the fulfilment of the whole life.'

45. Cf. page 51: '. . . the experience of life on the earth completes the making of the mind. In the *djinn* world the mind is only a design, an outline, a design which is not yet embroidered.'
    Cf. also page 121: 'There is no mind without body, for the body is the vehicle of the mind.'
    Cf. also page 123/124: '. . . the mind, before the body was made, was only an *ākāsha*. The experience it has gained through the body as its vehicle has become its knowledge, and it is this knowledge which makes the *ākāsha* mind.'

46. In a talk 'The Message is like rain' *(6th August, 1923)* Hazrat Inayat Khan had said: 'As the vapours which rise from the sea first and turn into clouds, so every aspect of knowledge gained by all beings rises upwards as vapours, forming into clouds as ideas, and again falling from above like rain.'

47. The relationship between body and mind, and body and soul is more amply explained in Part III; cf. page 171 and the illustration on page 172.

48. These five aspects of the mind are specified on page 121.

49. Ralph Waldo Emerson (1803 – 1882) was an American philosopher who wrote a study of the lives of the great men of humanity whom he considered representative of the various human characteristics.

50. The story of the magic tree occurs two times in the present edition, as Hazrat Inayat Khan told it twice in the course of his lectures.
    In Part II (page 118) the story illustrates the creative power of the mind, whereas in Part III (page 163/164) it gives a picture of the spirit world. Chronologically two months and a half separated the telling of the two tales, slightly different in some details.

51. *Māyā* is a term of Vedantic philosophy meaning: ignorance obscuring the vision of God; the cosmic illusion through which the One appears as many. In the present book Hazrat Inayat Khan spoke of 'mazing *māyā*'

NOTES

(page 118) and called it 'a puzzle' (page 127). It is possible that 'puzzle' meant to him a kind of maze. In a later series of lectures on 'The Purpose of Life' (Summer 1924) he spoke of 'a doll's puzzle', and told how difficult it had been for a fairy who had entered it, to find her way out again. (The published editions of the book show: 'a doll's house' – Chapter XIII).

52. '. . . the soul is like a mirror . . .'
Cf. page 37: 'The heart is a mirror. . .'
page 104: 'the body may be likened to a glass house made of mirrors.'
page 121: 'minds . . . may be likened to various mirrors.'

53. Some scholars assert that the word SUFI is derived from an Arabic word *sūf*, meaning wool, to denote that Sufis wear woollen garments. It is the view of others that this word is derived from the Arabic *safā*, meaning purity; in the Sufi conception this denotes: pure from differences and distinctions.

It is also considered that the word SUFI has relationship with the Greek word *sophia*, so that the word Sufism may convey the idea of that state which deals with the pursuit of divine wisdom.

(from 'The Way of Illumination' 1st edition)

54. *Dhāt*:
Cf. Inayat Khan's 'The Mysticism of Sound' – chapter 'The Silent Life':
'The life absolute from which has sprung all that is felt, seen and perceived, and into which all in time merges, is a silent motionless and eternal life, which among the Sufis is called *Dhāt*.'

55. *Dhāt and Ṣifat*:
Cf. Inayat Khan's 'The Unity of Religious Ideals' – chapter 'The Self and the Merit of God':
'In the terms of the Sufis the Self of God is called *Dhāt*, and His qualities, His merits are named *Ṣifat*. The Hindus call the former aspect of God *Purusha* and the latter *Prakriti*, which can be rendered in English by the words: Spirit and Nature.★
Dhāt, the Spirit of God is incomprehensible. The reason is that that which comprehends itself is Intelligence, God's real Being. . . .
Merit is something which is comprehensible; it is something which is clear and distinct: so it can be made intelligible. Intelligence is not intelligible – except to its own Self. Intelligence knows 'that I am'; but it does not know 'what I am'. Such is the Nature of God.'
Cf. also Inayat Khan's 'A Sufi Message of Spiritual Liberty' – chapter 'The Personal Being':
'Allah's★★ relation with Nature may be understood by analysing the idea expressed in the words: "I – Myself". This affirmation means the One Individual; at the same time it identifies the dual aspect of the One. In this phrase "I" is the Possessor, and "Myself" is the possessed. So also Allah (the Unmanifested) is the Possessor, and Nature (the

★Published editions of 'The Unity of Religious Ideals' show 'spirit and matter'.
★★In his earlier works Hazrat Inayat Khan used to say: Allah.

manifestation) is the possessed, which has its source hidden within itself.

The possessed could not have been created from anything other than the Possessor's own Self, as there existed none but the Possessor. Although the Possessor and the possessed are considered two separate entities, in reality they are one. The Possessor realizes the possessed through the medium of His own consciousness, which forms three aspects (Trinity) of the One Being.'

Cf. also the chapter 'Dual Aspect' in the same book:

'Dhāt projects Ṣifat from its own Self and absorbs it within itself. It is a philosophical rule that the positive cannot lose its positiveness by projecting the negative from itself, though the negative covers the positive within itself as the flame covers the fire. The negative has no independent existence, still it is real, because projected from the real; it may not be regarded as an illusion. Human ignorance persists in considering Dhāt separate from Ṣifat and Ṣifat independent of Dhāt.'*

56. Hazrat Inayat Khan explains that: as the seed produces the plant and is in turn produced by it, so Intelligence has caused the manifestation, and is again the outcome of it. Cf. Inayat Khan's GAYAN, Raga 22:

'O Thou, the seed of my life's plant, Thou wert hidden so long in my budlike soul; but now Thou hast come out, O my life's fruit, after the blossoming of my heart.'

57. Cf. Inayat Khan's "In an Eastern Rosegarden" – Chapter 'The Ideal Life': 'In the Hindu language the same word dharma means both duty and religion. Both are expressed by one word. "This is your dharma" (meaning: your faith) How beautiful the thought! Whatever kind of duty it is, so long as you have an ideal before you and are performing that duty, you are walking in the path of religion.'

58. Cf. Inayat Khan's 'The Way of Illumination' – Chapter 'Suma, the Music of the Sufis': 'There are different grades of progress, and the verses that are sung . . . are also of different kinds. Some verses are in the praise of the beauty of the ideal which the Sufis in the grade of fanā'-fi-Shaikh enjoy. In this grade are those who see the divine Immanence in the ideal walking on earth. There are verses which speak about the high merits of the ideal-in-name-and-not-in-form, which appeals to those who are in the grade of fanā'-fi-Rasūl. These have not seen the ideal, neither have they heard his voice, but they have known and loved that ideal which alone exists as far as they know. Then there are verses which speak about the ideal beyond name and form. To these verses those respond who are in the grade of fanā'-fi-Allah. These are conscious of their ideal as beyond name and form, qualities and merits, Who cannot even be confined in knowledge, being beyond all limitations.'

59. The following little story was omitted when 'The Soul – Whence and Whither' was first published and did not appear in subsequent editions. It is not known whether Hazrat Inayat Khan wished it to be left out.

*The French edition of this book, published one year before the English one, renders the correct words; in the English edition the words 'positive' and 'negative' are inverted.

NOTES

60. Hazrat Inayat Khan said originally that in Sufi terms purgatory might be called *kamāl*. (See Appendix, page 208 on Kamāl.) In the subsequent editions he revised this word.

61. Cf. page 122: 'It would not be an exaggeration if one called the mind a world: it is the world that man makes, in which he will make his life in the hereafter, as a spider weaves its web in which to live'.

62. Cf. page 52: 'Do the *djinns* communicate with the spirits returning from the earth?'

63. Transmigration of the soul – Hazrat Inayat Khan uses these words in a particular sense: a soul which has passed from the earth and which ought to be living in the spirit world 'migrates', removes from there back to the earth plane; it returns to a plane where it no longer belongs by taking possession of the body and mind of another soul living on the earth who then becomes as one 'living dead'. We are more accustomed to calling this 'obsession'. For Hazrat Inayat Khan, however, 'obsession in the true sense of the word' (cf page 155) is something natural; it means that an angel or a *djinn*, or a spirit focusses itself just for an instant upon the heart and mind of a person living on the earth, because a physical body with its organs of perception is needed in order to gain some knowledge from this plane. Often this may be called inspiration, especially in the case of an angel or a *djinn*.
    For 'obsession' by an angel see page 39.
    For 'obsession' by a *djinn* see page 59.
    For 'obsession' by a spirit see pages 145/146.
    When 'The Soul-Whence and Whither' was first published the words 'obsession' and 'impression' were used instead of the term 'transmigration of the soul', because this last was more generally understood to be much the same as reincarnation. However, the version adopted in the first edition and continued ever since has become obscured by this arrangement. If, on the contrary, Hazrat Inayat Khan's words are rightly understood in the sense he used them, they are perfectly clear and coherent.

64. 'Living dead in the good sense' – Speaking about the desire to live in 'The Purpose of Life' Hazrat Inayat Khan says: '. . . man wishes to live through the mortal part of his being; that is what brings disappointment. For he knows only that part of his being which is mortal and he identifies himself with his mortal being. Hardly one among a thousand realizes that life lives and death dies; that which lives cannot die; what dies will not live. . . . What is necessary, therefore, for a person is to make the spirit independent of the mortal covering, even if it be for a moment.'
    This last achievement is what is meant by 'to die before death', in other words: to be 'living dead in the good sense'.

65. Gopis are the milkmaids, companions and devotees of Shri Krishna, who passed his childhood with them at Vrindavan, a town on the banks of the Jamuna, a tributary of the river Ganges.

66. Hazrat 'Alī was the cousin and son-in-law of the Prophet Mohammed. He became the fourth Khalif of Islam.

67. The following short chapter, the subject of which belongs to the spirit

world or the sphere of the *djinns*, was added later to Hazrat Inayat Khan's original lectures. It was probably dictated by him. In the previous editions it is shown at the end of Part III.

68. Cf. page 95: 'Every soul that starts from the divine Sun vibrates differently.'

69. Cf. page 44/45: 'The enjoyment that the soul gets here on earth through the medium of the senses is like wine which just touches the lips. . . . There is only one pleasure which is real happiness. It does not belong to the earth.'

70. Intoxication – In a lecture given the 2nd December, 1923, in Paris, Hazrat Inayat Khan explained the meaning of 'intoxication' in greater depth:

'The higher intoxication cannot be compared with the lower intoxication of this world, but it is still intoxication. What is joy? What is fear? What is anger? What is passion? What is the feeling of attachment, and what is the feeling of detachment? All these give the same feeling of wine: all have their intoxications. Understanding this mystery the Sufis have founded their culture upon the principle of intoxication. They call this intoxication *ḥāl*. and *ḥāl* literally means condition or state. There is a Sufi saying: Man speaks and acts accordingly to his condition. One cannot speak or act differently from the wine one has drunk. With the one who has drunk the wine of anger, whatever he says or does is irritating; with the one who has drunk the wine of detachment, in his thought, speech and action you will find nothing but detachment; with the one who drinks the wine of attachment, you will find in his presence that all are drawn to him and that he is drawn to all. Everything a person does and says is according to the wine that he has taken. That is why the Sufi says: Heaven and hell are in the hand of man, if he only knew their mystery. To a Sufi the world is a wine-press; it is a store in which all sorts of wine are collected. He has only to choose what wine he will enjoy, and what wine will bring him the delight which is the longing of his soul.'

71. *Ṣawt-e-sarmad* – This is further explained in Inayat Khan's 'The Mysticism of Sound' – chapter 'Abstract Sound':

'The Sufis name it [the sound of the abstract] *sarmad*, which suggests the idea of intoxication. The word intoxication is here used to signify upliftment, the freedom of the soul from its earthly bondage. Those who are able to hear the *ṣawt-e-sarmad* and meditate on it, are relieved from all worries, anxieties, sorrows, fears and diseases, and the soul is freed from captivity in the senses and in the physical body.'

In the first part of this book – see page 43 – we are told that it was the intoxication produced by the singing of the angels which made the soul enter into the body of clay. The comparison of this intoxication to the one of *ṣawt-e-sarmad* illustrates Hazrat Inayat Khan's explanation of the different kinds of wine given in Note 70 above. Cf. also page 177: 'The farther the soul is removed from its source, the greater the intoxication.'

72. Cf. Hazrat Inayat Khan's explanation of Intelligence on page 128:

'The word intelligence, as it is known to us and spoken of in everyday language, does not give a full idea. . . . According to the mystic Intelligence is the primal element, or the cause as well as the effect.' See also note 40.

73. Hazrat Inayat Khan describes the bodies which the soul dons passing through the three planes of its existence in different ways:
Cf. page 53: ' . . . mankind is already dressed in the angelic dress over which he has put the dress of the *djinn*, and over the dress of the *djinn* he has put the dress of the human being. He really has all three dresses, one over the other'. Cf. also page 42: 'The soul in its nature is a current; the nature of this current is to envelop in itself all that may come along and meet it on its way.' Cf. also page 53: 'That secret current is the soul. Upon it is one globe over another. There is something within the body, but at the same time all is collected and gathered upon the current which is within'.
The Illustration of page 172, therefore, conveys an idea of the interpenetration of these different bodies, as well as of the way in which they cover one another.

74. See Forword, page 2, Hazrat Inayat Khan's letter to Miss J.E. Dowland.

75. *Fanā' and Baqā* – Cf. Hazrat Inayat Khan's 'The Purpose of Life' – Chapter IV: '*Fanā'* is not necessarily a destruction in God. *Fanā'* results in what may be called a resurrection in God, which is symbolized by the picture of Christ. The Christ on the cross is narrative of *fanā'*; it means: I am not. And the idea of resurrection explains the next stage which is *baqā*, and which means: Thou art.'

76. In 'The Phenomenon of the Soul' the same idea is expressed in the Conclusion:
'Since then I have seen all souls as my soul, and realized my soul as the soul of all; and what bewilderment it was when I realized that I alone was, if there was anyone, and that I am whatever and whoever there will be in the future. And there was no end to my happiness and joy.
Verily, I am the seed, and I am the root, and I am the fruit of this Tree of life.'

OTHER BOOKS
BY
HAZRAT INAYAT KHAN
MENTIONED IN THE TEXT

Most of the original books of Hazrat Inayat Khan were collected and republished for International Headquarters of the Sufi Movement (Geneva) by Barrie and Rockliff, London, between 1960 and 1969, in twelve volumes, as 'The Sufi Message of Hazrat Inayat Khan'. They are referred to below as SM. Vol. – .

1914   'A Sufi Message of Spiritual Liberty' (London)
      A French edition of this book was published in Paris in 1913.
      (The passage from 'Dual Aspect' cited in Note 55 is borrowed
      from this edition.)
      SM. Vol. V.

1918   'Hindustany Lyrics' (London).

1919   'Love, Human and Divine' (London)

1919   'The Phenomenon of the Soul' (London)
      The last two books given above were records of lectures by
      Hazrat Inayat Khan collected and written down by Sherifa
      Lucy Goodenough and published by her as 'The Voice of
      Inayat Series'. They were later republished in SM. Vol. V. In
      this three new chapters consisting of questions and answers
      raised at the lectures on 'The Soul-Whence and Whither' were
      added to the original text of 'The Phenomenon of the Soul'.

1922   'The Way of Illumination, A Guidebook to the Sufi Order,
      being compiled mainly from the writings of Inayat Khan,
      authorised edition' (London and Southampton, 2 editions).
      SM. Vol. I, with modifications and alterations.

about 1923   'The Mysticism of Sound' (London).
           Republished 1927 (London and Southampton).
           SM. Vol. II.

1927   'The Purpose of Life' (London).
      Republished 1973 (San Francisco).
      SM. Vol. I.

1931 'Character Building – The Art of Personality' (Plymouth)
SM. Vol. III.

about 1932 'The Unity of Religious Ideals' (London).
Republished 1949 (Deventer, Netherlands).
Republished 1979 (New York).
SM. Vol. IX – with alterations and additions.

1939 'Three Plays' (Deventer, Netherlands)
SM. Vol. XII.

1956 'Philosophy, Psychology, Mysticism' (Zaandijk,
Netherlands).
SM. Vol. XI.

1979 'Biography of Pir-o-Murshid Inayat Khan' (East-West
Publications London and The Hague).

SOURCES AND DOCUMENTS USED IN COMPILING THE TEXT

Miss J.E.D. Furnee (Sakina)★

(1) A shorthand report covering most of the lectures, together with the questions and answers.

(2) Some loose and very incomplete typewritten sheets which could be her transcriptions from her own shorthand. (They have been corrected in her handwriting).

(3) A new transcription of her shorthand report made by the staff members of the Foundation Nekbakht Stichting, (Miss Furnee used the Pond Shorthand system of The Hague, Netherlands, and applied it as a rule both accurately and legibly.)

Miss L. Goodenough (Murshida Sherifa)★

(1) A longhand report covering the greater part of the series of lectures, in most cases identical with Miss Furnee's report – also a good proportion of the questions and answers exchanged after the lectures. (It should be noted here that Inayat Khan used to speak slowly; his words could be noted down in longhand while he spoke.)

(2) A number of neatly written records of lectures originally given under the title "Metaphysics". Some of these are probably original reports.

(3) Loose typewritten sheets recording lectures on "Metaphysics" on which there are corrections made in Miss Goodenough's handwriting.

(4) A copy of "The Soul – Whence and Whither?", 1st edition, with many amendments inscribed by her. The book held in the archives is not the original but is one in which the alterations were copied out by Miss A. van der Scheer (Feisi)★, who acted as secretary to Miss L. Goodenough.

Mrs. G. Lloyd (Kefayat)★

(1) A longhand report noted down while Inayat Khan spoke containing a great number of lectures with relevant questions and answers. Barring some errors and inexactitudes these reports are fairly reliable. Some of the pages contain corrections and additions in Miss E.M. Green's handwriting.

(2) A special note-book in which was entered a fair copy of the questions and answers – sometimes more or less corrected by herself.

Mr. H.P. Baron van Tuyll van Serooskerken and Mrs. H. Baroness van Tuyll van Serooskerken (Sirdar and Saida)★

(1) A record of many of the lectures with relevant questions and answers, taken'down by one or other of them in the same note-book.

(2) Records of questions and answers without the lectures which gave rise to them. Some of the lectures and of the questions and answers may have been direclty reported at the time, and others copied out later. There is no doubt that the Baron had access to Mrs. Lloyd's note-books as in some instances he filled in words which had been left blank.

Miss E.M. Saintsbury Green (Murshida Sophia)★

(1) A number of questions and answers for publication in the magazine "Sufism" in the preparation of which Mrs. Lloyd's report was used. Only some of these were actually published. The documents held in the archives are incomplete.

(2) Corrections and additions entered in Mrs. G. Lloyd's note-books. (See above.)

(3) One sentence written on a separate sheet, mentioned in Note 8.

Mrs. C. van Spengler (Kemila)*

A handwritten record of many questions and answers and of some of the lectures copied by her in London in about 1930 from papers in the possession of Miss M. Williams (Zohra)*, one of Inayan Khan's first English pupils.

Some loose typewritten sheets containing lectures. The origin of these sheets cannot be determined. They were kept in the archives and bear no handwritten additions.

Copies of the 1st and 2nd editions of "The Soul – Whence and Whither?"

---

* Hazrat Inayat Khan gave these names. They are mentioned here because they occur in the archives of the Foundation Nekbakht Stichting.

SUBJECT INDEX

Accommodation or Akasha or Asman: 9, 10, 12, 102, 103; centres of inner perception, 107, 108; the eye, 66, 67, 113; the heart, 66, 80; the mind, 48, 67, 88, 89, 91/92, 111, 112, 113, 115, 117, 123/124; the organs of the senses, 102, 104; the soul, 90.

Angels, different kinds: 9 kinds 32, 35, 36; "fallen", 24; farishta, 24; guardian 33, 34; Khayr and Khar, 34; malak, 20; male and female, 29; recording 34, 36; suras, 20, 168; of death, 30, 31, 32; of jalal and jamal, 35; of nur and of nar, 35.

mentioned by name: Cupid, 43, 71; Gabriel 30/31, 36; Iblis, 42/43, 46; Lucifer 47; Munkir and Nakir 35.

characteristics: playing harps, 21, 96; are flames, 26, 38; are made of light, 23, 26, 38, 174; are near to God, 20; are vibrations, 21, 96; birth and death, 40; the body, 82, 174, the form, 23, 24, 30; the language, 30/31.

and spirits: 24, 32

and human beings: scarcity of relations, 21, 29, 36; who remain angels and who become human beings, 22, 38/39; who help human beings 30, 35/36, 39 See also Guardian angel; produced by the virtues of human beings, 38; man greater, 20.

Angelic Heavens, or angelic spheres: 20, 25, 38, 42, 84; life in the, 64, 84, 169, 173; music in the, 43, 169, 170; homesickness or longing for the, 26, 71/72, 173; the soul's occupation in the, 169, 173.

Angelic quality in man: 21, 25, 26, 28, 81.

Annihiliation: 20, 132, 178, 190.

Artificiality of life: 102, 107, 109, 202.

Atoms: are living beings, 17, have a consciousness, 186; have a soul, 41; of the physical body, 88, 152, 186; collected by the soul, 38, 53; different on every plane, 54; set into motion, 108; appearing, 15.

Aura: 21, 110.

Bible: New Testament, 42, 119, 131, 195, 200; Old Testament or ancient Scriptures 24, 29, 35, 51, 82, 111, 162/163.

Body: 102-110; see also Mind and body; see also Soul and body; qualities: the four qualities, 98; an offering from the universe, 74; dependent on the climate, 91; needs breath, 108; the intelligence of the 171; a glass house, 104; the temple of God, 104.

looking after the, 104, 105; death of the, 135, 152, 153.

Breath: see also God's breath; definitions and characteristics: – or nur, 109; or prana, 54, 57; or sura, 20; the great, 16; the mystery of, 71; inhaling and exhaling, 15, 17, 18, 19, 20, 114; is the ego, 38; is life, 54; is a rosary, 19; is like a river, 57; is creative, 17, 18.

– and the body, 107, 108; – and the soul, 19, 42, 135; – and kamal, 208.

Consciousness: see also God's consciousness; of existence, 1; silent, 11; God-, 93, 95, 130, 131; God- and self-,

INDEX

INDEX

INDEX

Holy Spirit, or Holy Ghost: 31, 168.

Spirits: 24, 112; communicating with, 155; spirits communicating or being connected with people on earth, 146, 147, 154/155, 160; communicating with one another, 167; communicating with djinns, 52, 146, 169; communicating with angels, 26, 169.

nature spirits, 33; evil spirits, 24.

Spirit World: life in the, 160, 165, 166, 167; picture of the, 160.

Spirituality: the only object of human evolution, 41; the development of the angelic quality, 26.

Stories: of the fairy who took her lover to the Court of Indra, 26/27; of Iblis refusing to bow before man, 42/43; of Krishna dancing with the Gopis, 160; of the Murshid, the murîd and the mad dog, 199; of the simpleton who thought he was dead, 137/138; of the soul afraid to enter the body of clay, 43; of the magic tree, 118, 163/164.

Sufi: – and Yogi, 93, 105, 106/107, 109, 205-207.

– terminology, 9, 10, 34, 104, 157, 169, 173.

quotations from Sufi poets and sages: 38, 106, 127, 190, 194; see also Kabir, Omar Khayyam, Shams Tabriz, Rumi.

Sufism: the word, 125/126; is the analysing of self, 126; the process of unlearning, 127; teaches the love for God, 93,206.

Suicide: 136.

Time: see also Space and time.

three kinds of, 68; in this world and in the next, 41, 140, 166, 190; time or years spent in the djinn sphere and in the angelic Heavens, 64, 65, 174, 190; that man knows and God's eternal life, 16; does not exist, 83, 189.

Trinity: 11/12, 128.

Truth: the ultimate, 68, 113; the knowledge of, 131, 138; the greatest religion, 131, 179; cannot be put into words, 76, 128; is that which is discovered, 78.

Unity, Variety, plurality: see also Duality.

11/12, 28, 32, 40, 78, 93, 150, 165.

Vibration: the laws of, 9, 84, 96/97.

the angel is –, 21, 96; the soul is –, 168; caused by the repetition of a sacred word, 108.

Words: becoming tongues of flame, 30; sacred –, 108; the word that was lost, 103, 110.

INDEX OF PROPER NAMES

INDEX

INDEX of WORDS in ORIENTAL LANGUAGES

The vocabulary of the mystics contains many Arabic words which are also found in the Persian and Urdu languages. In these the final letter 'h' is then often changed into a 't'. Hazrat Inayat Khan used this Persian/Urdu ending for some words, for others he used the pure Arabic form. E.g. *aḥadiyyat and ammarah.*

The Arabic spelling has been adopted in the text for all words of Arabic origin.

The terms used by Hazrat Inayat Khan are explained by him in their context.

(Note . . . refers to terms mentioned only in the Notes)

Ar. = Arabic   P. = Persian   Skt. = Sanskrit

āb P. 10.
aḥadiyyah Ar. 9.
a'ina Khana P. 104.
ajsām Ar. 9, 10.
ākāsha Skt. see Subject-Index.
calimah Ar. 95.
ammarah Ar. 94.
apsara Skt. 52.
arwah Ar. 9, 10.
asmān P. 9, 108.
carsh Ar. 21.
asura Skt. 20, 24, 168.
ātesh P. 10.
ātmā Skt. 125.
bād P. 10.
bāgh P. 128.
bahār P. 128.
baqā Ar. 178.
bhakti Skt. 205.
bulbul Ar. 128.
chaitanya Skt. 15.
dēva Skt. 32, 33.
dharma Skt. 130.
dhāt Ar. 9, 127, 128.
djinn Ar. see Subject-Index.
fanā' Ar. 132, 148, 178.
farishta P. 24.
gāndhārva Skt. 52.
ghawth Ar. 32.
gōpī Skt. 160.
hāhūt Ar. 92.
ḥāl Ar. Note 70.
insān Ar. 9.
jabarūt Ar. 92, 93.
jalāl Ar. 35, 208.
jamāl Ar. 35, 208.

jannat Ar. 141.
jīvan mukta Skt. 192.
jnāna Skt. 48.
kamāl 208–209.
karmā Skt. 81, 157, 188, 195, 196.
kawthar Ar. 169.
khāk P. 10.
khalīfah Ar. 88.
khayr Ar. 34.
khār P. 34.
lahūt Ar. 92.
lawwāmah Ar. 94.
loka Skt. 52 and Note 32.
malak Ar. 20.
malakūt Ar. 91, 92, 93.
manas Skt. 80, 116.
māyā Skt. 118, 127.
mukti Skt. 196, 197.
Munkir Ar. 35.
murīd Ar. 106, 158, 199, 200, 204.
Murshid Ar. 198, 199, 200, 204.
mutma'innah Ar. 94.
nabī Ar. 32.
nafs Ar. 38, 39, 94.
najāt Ar. 197.
Nākir Ar. 35.
nār Ar. 35.
nāsūt Ar. 91, 92, 93.
nazā' Ar. 141.
naẓar Ar. 128.
nirvana Skt. 86, 87, 88.
nūr Ar. 9, 10, 26, 35, 38, 54, 108.
pala Skt. 16.
prakriti Skt. Note 55.
pralaya Skt. 15.
prāna Skt. 54, 57.

239

INDEX